STANLEY
COOKBOOK
ANNE CAIN

STANLEY COOKBOOK

ANNE CAIN

Design: Bridgewater Design
Photography: Hilary Moore
Styling: Philomena O'Neill
Food preparation for photography: Sandra Baddeley
Typesetting: Mark Tennent
Printed and bound in Italy by Printer Trento

Published by Martin Books
Simon & Schuster Consumer Group
Grafton House 64 Maids Causeway
Cambridge CB5 8DD

in association with Waterford Stanley Ltd
Bilberry
Waterford
Republic of Ireland

First published 1992
© Martin Books 1992
ISBN 0 85941 820 0

Contents

Introduction

INTRODUCING A SUPER STAR

You are now the proud owner of a traditional cast iron Stanley Super Star that is capable of providing full central heating and domestic hot water, as well as fulfilling all your cooking requirements with two ovens having separate controls for cooking and heating topped with a spacious hotplate with rapid boiling facility. Your first step is to familiarize yourself with all the different ways in which the Super Star can be adapted to work for you.

The Super Star is a combined full central heating system and a cooker. The main oven works just like a conventional oven in that it has its own thermostat which brings it to the required heat in 15–20 minutes and the heat rises, giving you different heat zones to bake in. However, this cooker has more to offer than a conventional oven.

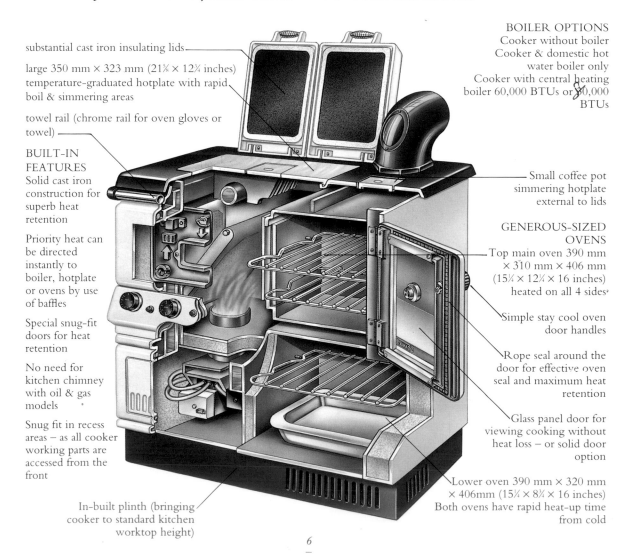

substantial cast iron insulating lids

large 350 mm × 323 mm (21⅜ × 12¾ inches) temperature-graduated hotplate with rapid boil & simmering areas

towel rail (chrome rail for oven gloves or towel)

BUILT-IN FEATURES
Solid cast iron construction for superb heat retention

Priority heat can be directed instantly to boiler, hotplate or ovens by use of baffles

Special snug-fit doors for heat retention

No need for kitchen chimney with oil & gas models

Snug fit in recess areas – as all cooker working parts are accessed from the front

In-built plinth (bringing cooker to standard kitchen worktop height)

BOILER OPTIONS
Cooker without boiler
Cooker & domestic hot water boiler only
Cooker with central heating boiler 60,000 BTUs or 80,000 BTUs

Small coffee pot simmering hotplate external to lids

GENEROUS-SIZED OVENS
Top main oven 390 mm × 310 mm × 406 mm (15¼ × 12¼ × 16 inches) heated on all 4 sides

Simple stay cool oven door handles

Rope seal around the door for effective oven seal and maximum heat retention

Glass panel door for viewing cooking without heat loss – or solid door option

Lower oven 390 mm × 320 mm × 406mm (15¼ × 8¾ × 16 inches) Both ovens have rapid heat-up time from cold

OPERATING THE STANLEY SUPER STAR 60,000 B.T.U. MODEL

The heat source, be it natural gas, LPG or oil fired, incorporates a pressure jet type of burner system which allows the cooker to switch off when the selected temperature is achieved, saving unnecessary fuel expense. (Another economical feature of your Super Star is that there is no pilot light or wick demanding a 24-hour fuel supply.) Directly above the burner hang the baffles, which direct the heat to the source you have chosen by selecting a particular working mode. The temperature is selected at the control panel.

THE CONTROL PANEL

The control panel is simplicity itself. The major controls are the thermostats - one for the central heating and one for the oven. As a safety precaution, the high-limit thermostat button will trip out if the thermostat settings are exceeded. There is also an indicator light (or lights, depending on which model you have purchased) which will indicate when the burner is running and if it has reached the selected temperature. A lock-out light will come on in the unlikely event of a burner failing to ignite. The heat baffles are controlled by rotating the control knobs with the operating tool provided.

TO SELECT THE CENTRAL HEATING MODE

Turn the oven thermostat to idle. With the right-hand baffle vertical, turn the left-hand baffle control knob (under the image of a radiator) anti-clockwise, using the operating tool provided. Set the boiler thermostat to the required setting.

TO SELECT THE OVEN MODE

Turn the central heating thermostat to idle. With the left-hand baffle vertical, turn the right-hand baffle control knob (under the image of a roasting chicken) clockwise, using the operating tool provided. Set the oven thermostat to the required cooking temperature.

TO SELECT THE HOTPLATE MODE

Turn the boiler thermostat to idle. Ensure that both baffles are vertical and then set the oven thermostat to the desired level.

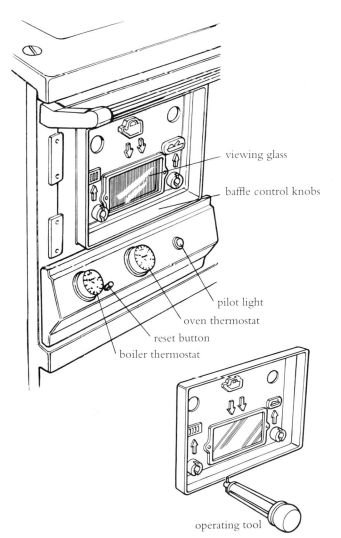

viewing glass

baffle control knobs

pilot light

oven thermostat

reset button

boiler thermostat

operating tool

THE CENTRAL HEATING MODE

The baffles will direct the heat initially to the boiler, next up to the hotplate (giving adequate heat for hotplate cooking) and then on to the main oven. This mode will give you gallons of domestic hot water and sufficient heat for up to 12 radiators. The transference of heat into the main oven will give it a temperature of up to 200°C after a couple of hours, depending on the number of radiators in use, while the lower oven will be approximately half as hot. You can see from this that if you suddenly need the oven while the Super Star is set in the central heating mode it will not take very long for the main oven to reach maximum temperature. Just switch to the cooking mode, set the oven thermostat to your requirements and within minutes you are ready to cook. Remember to switch back to the central heating mode when you no longer require extra heat to the oven.

THE OVEN MODE

The baffles are now directing the heat towards the main oven and the unique design of the Stanley Super Star allows this heat to transfer right around the oven on all four sides before travelling through to the flue. There is still sufficient boiler exposed in this position to satisfy domestic hot water requirements. The fact that the main oven is heated equally on all four faces means it will cook the food evenly. The lower oven absorbs the heat from the middle flueway to the top section of the lower oven, and will give you a temperature approximately half that of the main oven thermostat setting, enabling you to utilise this extra heated space accordingly. As with the central heating mode, there is adequate heat to the hotplate for most hotplate cooking.

THE HOTPLATE MODE

The baffles are now directing the heat upward to the hotplate then on to the main oven, the flue gases again satisfying domestic hot water requirements. This mode will give you an approximate temperature of 200°C in the main oven and 100°C in the lower oven. (Of course, you can demand a higher temperature by setting the cooker to oven mode.) Using this working mode at breakfast gives you a very fast heat-up time suitable for every household – even the one that oversleeps! The graded hotplate has an extra-rapid boiling facility – and, although the main thrust of heat is being directed to the hotplate, just look at the temperature you are getting in the main oven! Grilling and breakfast cooking can also be done using the grill rack in the main oven – see Main Oven section (page 11).

Now you know the three working modes of your Super Star you will realize how versatile this appliance is. Heat is there whenever the system is working, to be utilized and adapted accordingly. Changing the operating mode of the cooker is not complicated – there are only three movements to make, no more than if you were using a microwave.

OPERATING THE STANLEY SUPER STAR 90,000 B.T.U. MODEL

SETTING A
HIGH OUTPUT BOILER MODE

WATER/CENTRAL HEATING

hotplate baffle control knob

1 Set oven temperature to idle.
2 Lift and slide the boiler baffle control knob to the left until it locks into position.
3 Swing the hotplate baffle control knob to the right.
4 Open by-pass damper.
5 Set the boiler thermostat as required to control hotplate temperature.

damper open

boiler baffle control knob

SETTING B
HIGH HOT PLATE AND OVEN OUTPUT
MODE WITH REDUCED BOILER OUTPUT

COOKING

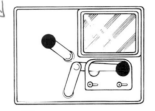

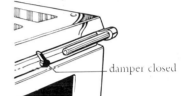

1 Set oven thermostat to idle
2 Swing the hotplate baffle control knob to the left.
3 Lift and slide the boiler baffle control knob to the right until it locks into position.
4 Close by-pass damper.
5 Set the boiler thermostat as required to control hotplate temperature.

damper closed

THIS ONE & REMEMBER

SETTING C
HIGH OVEN OUTPUT MODE WITH HOT
PLATE AND LOW BOILER OUTPUT

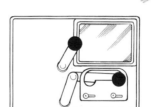

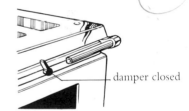

1 Set boiler thermostat to idle.
2 Lift and slide the boiler baffle control knob to the right until it locks into position.
3 Swing the hotplate baffle control knob to the right.
4 Close the by-pass damper.
5 Set the oven thermostat to the required cooking temperature.

damper closed

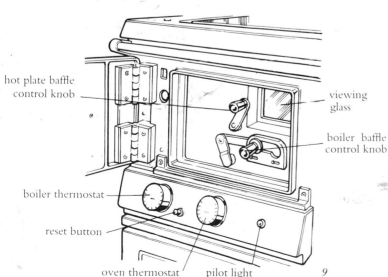

hot plate baffle control knob

viewing glass

boiler baffle control knob

boiler thermostat

reset button

oven thermostat   pilot light

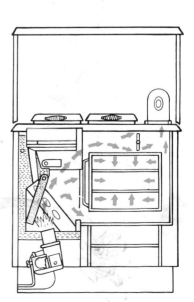

THE AUTOMATIC TIMESWITCH

Most people will operate the central heating system by the automatic timeswitch, which enables the heating to switch itself on and off at pre-set times. It is sheer luxury to get up in the morning to find the central heating has been on for about an hour, there is plenty of hot water, and the kettle, left on the simmering plate overnight, is nearly boiling. For economy, the system can be set to switch off after breakfast when perhaps most members of the family have left the house and to come on again from late afternoon until bedtime. If the oven is required during the day, simply override the clock control/automatic timeswitch, set the cooker to the oven mode and use. The oven will reach the required temperature in just 20 minutes.

The automatic timeswitch can also be used to bring the oven on while you are out of the house. It can also be set to switch the oven off so that food will not be overcooked if you come home later than you expected.

SUMMER RUNNING

While your Super Star will give you lots of winter warmth, it will not overheat the kitchen in summer. The thermostatically controlled oven can be on for as short or as long a time as you require during the summer months with no wastage of heat. If the summer does bring a few chilly evenings, just switch to the central heating mode for one or two hours to take the chill off the house – and do not forget your central heating boiler thermostat can be set a little lower in the summer to be more economical if you so wish.

WINTER RUNNING

In the cold winter months you may need to have the cooker operating almost continuously during the day on the central heating mode, so what about cooking? Remember the heat transference into the main oven which is giving you a temperature of up to 200°C.

Imagine a day during very cold weather. Before retiring the night before, you will have placed the kettle on the simmering hotplate and mixed the porridge, covered it and placed it in the main oven. Approximately one hour before the household wakes up the cooker switches on to the central heating mode. There is a lovely warm kitchen to come down to at breakfast, after a hot shower. The cooker is switched to the hotplate mode for a fast breakfast. After breakfast, as most members of the household leave to go their separate ways, the cooker is switched back to the central heating mode to keep the house comfortably warm and well supplied with hot water. During breakfast the oven temperature will have reached 200°C. Make full use of this by preparing a casserole with all that heat on the hotplate and then transfer it to the oven. It will be ready by lunchtime, but if your main meal is not required until the end of the day you can adapt the oven heat accordingly – if the casserole is cooking too quickly, transfer it to the lower oven for a longer cooking period (and perhaps add some potatoes for baking). All sorts of sweet and savoury dishes can be prepared and cooked during the day while the Super Star is on the central heating mode, ready for the family at the end of a busy day. If you require more heat to the oven towards the end of the day, simply switch to the oven mode.

THE STANLEY MULTI FUEL MODEL

The Multi Fuel Model completes the superb range of Stanley Super Star central heating cookers. Being a true multi-fuel appliance it will burn household coal, seasoned wood, peat, or any of the smokeless-type fuels. Boasting an automatic thermostat, with manual override, together with a mid-boiler summer grate position, the cooker is an all-year-round performer.

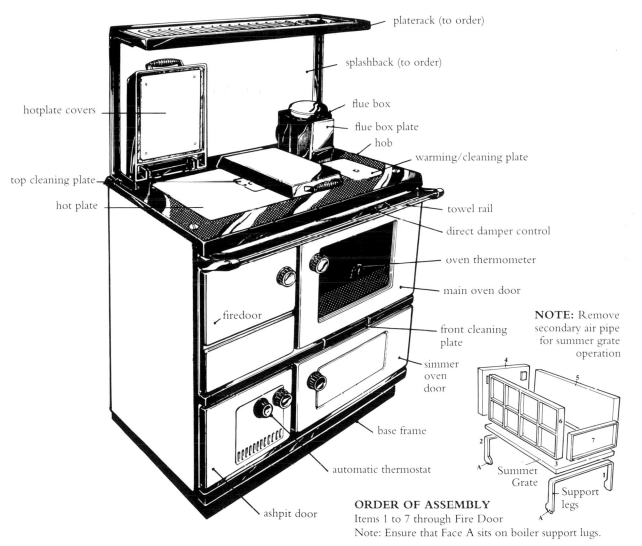

platerack (to order)

splashback (to order)

flue box

flue box plate

hob

warming/cleaning plate

hotplate covers

top cleaning plate

hot plate

towel rail

direct damper control

oven thermometer

main oven door

firedoor

front cleaning plate

simmer oven door

base frame

automatic thermostat

ashpit door

NOTE: Remove secondary air pipe for summer grate operation

Summer Grate

Support legs

ORDER OF ASSEMBLY
Items 1 to 7 through Fire Door
Note: Ensure that Face A sits on boiler support lugs.

ACCESSORIES SUPPLIED
summer grate, tools, roasting or baking tin

SUMMER GRATE & HEAT SHIELDS
To obtain a reduction in boiler output during the summer the Cooker is supplied with a removable summer grate and cast iron heat shield plates as standard.

Remove the existing grate and stand the summer grate on the supporting legs after inserting it through the firedoor. Fit heat shield plates as shown in diagram.

THE MAIN OVEN

The main oven is a generous size at 39 × 31 × 40 cm (15 × 12 × 16 inches), big enough to take a 12 kg (28 lb) turkey. It is a cast iron construction which gives a perfect roast, sealing in the natural juices and flavours and minimizing shrinkage. Any food spillage in the main oven will be burnt off at a high temperature and all you have to do when the oven has cooled is brush it out with a stiff brush. What could be simpler? The double-glazed door enables you to see how cooking is progressing without losing heat by opening the door, and there is a heat indicator set in the glass which is a secondary check on your oven temperature. The door seal is very effective and the door handle is made of bakelite, a heat-resistant material, so it does not get hot. There are four shelf positions and since the heat rises, as with all conventional ovens, you will find the top shelf position hotter than the bottom shelf.

This top shelf position is good for grilling, and there is a grill rack for the roasting tin. For a delicious breakfast, lightly grease the base of the roasting tin (a well-seasoned tin will not need this) and place in it slices of bread with a hole cut out of the centre, using a pastry cutter. Carefully crack a whole egg into the hole. Place the grilling rack over the eggs and lay bacon and sausage on the rack – the fat will drop out of the meat on to the eggs, helping to cook and flavour them.

Mushrooms and tomatoes may also be cooked in the roasting tin, and fish, especially fillets, grills excellently this way. Unlike a conventional cooker, the Super Star transmits heat all around the sides of the oven so you can cook on the base of the main oven – marvellous for quiches and other pastry recipes, which come out of the oven with a crisp base. The main oven is also ideal for shallow-frying in cast iron cookware, and all oven smells will pass directly out of the cooker via the flue – no cooking smells in the kitchen but, remember, no burning smells either!

This diagram illustrates how the baffles direct the heat towards and around all four faces of the main oven when the cooker is in the cooking mode. Heat is, of course, transferred to the lower oven at this time and domestic water supply is also adequately provided.

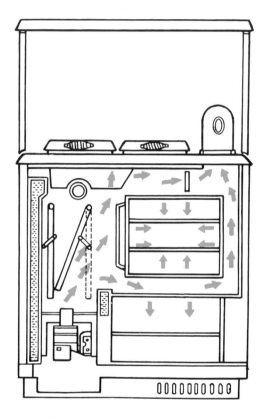

THE LOWER OVEN

The lower oven is a sealed unit of 39 × 22 × 40 cm (15 × 9 × 16 inches) with two oven shelf positions. It operates at approximately half the main oven temperature. As the heat is transferred downwards from the main oven, the top shelf position of the lower oven is hotter than the bottom shelf. Like the main oven, it has a cast iron interior and gives a similarly superb cooked finish to those dishes that require a more delicate heat source. Long, slow cooking is as good in this oven as the main oven. This is an ideal place to put the roast to rest before carving, to slow up vegetables or other foods that are cooking too quickly, and to keep food warm without drying out for latecomers. It is also marvellous for meringues and milk puddings. There is plenty of storage space for baking utensils and it is ideal for warming serving dishes, plates and jars or bottles when you are preserving. When you are making bread, it provides a handy place for dough to rise out of draughts. It has the same self-clean oven facilities as the main oven.

THE HOTPLATE

One of the outstanding features of the Stanley Super Star is its hotplate. It makes full use of the top of the cooker, with an additional small simmering plate on the right-hand side. This generous hotplate is machine ground for maximum heat transfer to the cookware. It measures 55 × 33 cm (22 × 13 inches) and is graded in temperature, the hottest section being to the left. This is due to the cast iron fins which hang vertically from the underside of the hotplate so the greater mass of cast iron retains the heat. Both hotplates are easy to keep clean, and it is effortless to slide saucepans along the surface to obtain the correct cooking temperature you require. Five saucepans can be fitted on to the hotplate – one 20 cm (8 inches), two 19 cm (7½ inches), one 15 cm (6 inches) and one 14 cm (5½ inches). The twin insulating covers conserve the heat that would otherwise be lost into the kitchen to give you instant heat when required – lift one or both at a time. Stir-frying is easy on this surface and, lightly oiled, it is simple to griddle on, to make drop scones, griddle cakes, scotch pancakes or burgers.

The small simmering plate is ideal for keeping the coffee pot warm or a kettle full of water ready to move on to the hotplate when required. All sorts of culinary jobs can be done near this gentle heat – dissolving gelatine, melting butter, fats and chocolate, warming

liquids for doughmaking. The list is endless.

COOKING UTENSILS

You do not have to buy a new set of pans when you take delivery of your Stanley cooker, but it is advisable to check your cookware. Thin, lightweight saucepans are liable to buckle under extreme heat, so it is therefore recommended that you use saucepans with a heavy thermic base, giving complete contact with the hotplate for fast, even distribution of the heat and maximum heat retention for a good cooking performance.

Some Continental saucepans of 18/20 stainless steel are designed with a 5.5 mm thermic base, using a core of aluminium sandwiched between two layers of stainless steel which is then bonded to the base of the saucepan. The aluminium does not come into contact with the food while cooking. Other Continental designs are of a 5-ply construction from base to lip. This construction consists of an inner and outer layer of Inox stainless steel for toughness and durability and an inner sandwich of aluminium and aluminium alloy to provide a good dispersion of heat, not only at the base but up the sides as well.

Many manufacturers of stainless steel saucepans now produce a range of oven-to-table ware, with handles and knobs of matching stainless steel. These pans enable you to start cooking a recipe on the hotplate, transfer to the oven with no heat damage to lid or handle, and then serve at the table. Certain manufacturers produce a full and attractive range of different-sized saucepans, casseroles and straight-sided stockpots, enabling you to purchase your own mix and match set.

Many people prefer the look and feel of cast iron cookware. These pans are just as versatile as stainless steel saucepans, absorbing and distributing the heat evenly and going from the hotplate to the oven and then to the table. They are available in a range of designs and colours. Although good-quality saucepans can

be expensive, the versatility they offer means that fewer items need be purchased for hotplate cooking.

Ovenproof earthenware and glass dishes will produce satisfactory results from this cooker. Your traditional cake tins, baking sheets, loaf tins and any other favourite ovenware you use will be suitable, while a roasting tin and grill rack are provided.

You can use a pressure cooker on the hotplate. The graduated heat will assist you greatly, for when a certain pressure is reached you can merely slide the pressure cooker along to a cooler part of the hotplate. However, do check that the base of the pressure cooker is even in order to make a good contact with the hotplate.

THE CARE OF YOUR COOKER

The luxurious glow of the Super Star's vitreous enamel finish will complement any design of kitchen, be it modern or traditional, and one of the main assets of this cooker is the small amount of cleaning it requires.

Vitreous enamel is tough and long-lasting but should be treated with care. Acidic spills on the hob should be wiped off immediately with a damp cloth. The vitreous enamel front, sides

and hob only need a wipe with a warm soapy cloth then a polish with a dry cloth. Do not use an abrasive cleaning material on the vitreous enamel; if there is a stubborn mark, use a proprietary cream to remove it, following the instructions carefully. The hotplate will carbonize any food spilt on it, which should then be brushed away with a wire brush. This will ensure a good contact between cooking utensil and the hotplate. The twin insulating covers should be washed on the outside with a warm soapy cloth and then dried and polished with a clean dry cloth. (Take care when cleaning the insulating covers – the hotplate may be hot.) The ovens are self-cleaning in that any food that spills on the oven interior will carbonize and can then be brushed away. Keep the glass door clean by wiping with a warm soapy cloth and then drying with a dry cloth.

SERVICING

We recommend that the cooker and burner be serviced by an authorized service agent engineer. Provided that the cooker has been operated normally the burner and cooker flueways will only need servicing approximately every 6 to 12 months.

The Stanley Super Star can be fuelled by

natural gas, LPG or oil. Although they all work on the same principle, every cooker's efficiency and performance will vary a little according to site conditions, draught particulars and pipe layouts.

GENERAL INFORMATION

The Stanley Super Star cooker becomes part of the family so quickly it is hard to imagine how you managed without one. It is not only a versatile heat centre, it combines durability and elegance, and is so streamlined it blends into any kitchen design.

During the winter months, when the weather is very cold, the central heating mode will no doubt be running for many hours to create a comfortable home. If there is a newborn member in the family and you have to get up in the middle of the night, how comforting it is to walk into a warm kitchen, with a kettle sitting on the simmering plate to assist you with the speedy preparation of baby's bottle. And as the children grow, so do the

demands on the cooker as it is used to warm wellington boots and outdoor garments before they venture out to play on a winter's day, and to dry paintings, models and pottery shapes.

If the design of your kitchen allows, a ceiling-fixed drier over the cooker is a very handy piece of equipment. The drier can be used for drying and airing clothes - often a mammoth task for a young and active family. (If you have the optional plate rack, it could double up to air the clothes in an emergency.) You can also use the drier to hang up bunches of flowers, too, to dry, for craft use or just for decoration.

STANLEY STAR TIPS

You will soon come to look upon the Stanley as a reliable companion to help you during a busy baking session or when you are preparing that extra-special meal. The following tips are ways in which I have found the Stanley invaluable; no doubt you will quickly add discoveries of your own to the list.

1. Baking: If you are using butter or margarine from the refrigerator, simply place the required amount of fat in a heatproof bowl on the hob, near to the hotplate. It will be quickly brought to room temperature, making it easier to work with.

2. Breadmaking: Stand the required liquid for the recipe in a heatproof jug on the hob near the hotplate to warm. Take care not to overheat as yeast is killed at high temperatures.

3. Breadmaking: Depending on what mode the cooker is set at, the hob, plate rack or lower oven can be used for proving the dough.

4. Baking: To dissolve gelatine, place two tablespoons of water or liquid from the recipe in a small heatproof bowl. Sprinkle the required amount of gelatine on the liquid and place on or near the hotplate to dissolve. A small stainless steel bowl is useful for this type of job.

5. Baking: When melted chocolate is needed in a recipe or for decoration work, simply place the chocolate in a heatproof bowl near the hotplate. This method is easier than placing over a pan of hot water, which can often splash into the chocolate and spoil it.

6. Baking: Syrup tins and jam jars with only a little left in them are easier to empty when they have warmed on the hob.

7. Cooking: If a recipe requires a small amount of fried or softened onion, place the finely chopped onion and a little butter or oil in a heatproof bowl on or near the hotplate to soften. I use this method often, because it is so much easier than having to wash up a frying-pan! Many different types of vegetables can be prepared this way before adding to a recipe.

8. Cooking: To make breadcrumbs, simply place the bread on a baking sheet in the lower oven and allow to dry out. Crush and store for future use.

9. Cooking: To make croûtons, cut the bread into small cubes, place in a shallow cast iron dish with a little oil and fry, using the base of the main oven. (If the oven is not in use, fry on the hotplate.) Drain, spread out on a baking sheet and put to crisp in the lower oven. Croûtons can be frozen for use when required.

10. Drying: An abundance of fresh herbs need not be wasted. Place on a baking sheet, after washing and patting dry with kitchen paper, and leave to dry in the lower oven. Store for future use.

11. Drying: Cooked rice can be spread out on a baking sheet and left to dry in the lower oven.

12. Baking: When making fruit cakes, wash the dried fruit, place on a baking sheet and allow to dry off in the lower oven before use. Moist fruit will sink to the bottom of a cake and spoil it.

13. Preserving: When you are bottling, the depth of the main oven makes it easy to sit a tray of bottled fruit all on the same shelf to cook in one session.

14. Preserving: When you are making jam the graduated hotplate enables you to control the simmering of a large preserving pan much more easily than on a conventional cooker, where the pan is too large for the burner or ring. The warming of sugar, drying of the prepared fruit and the warming of jars and bottles can all be done with plenty of space using the lower oven and plate rack, if you have one.

ROASTING CHART

All timings are guidelines only, as there are no set rules for roasting meat – each cut lends itself to several different ways of preparation and cooking and each family will have a personal preference. When meat is roasted quickly the juices are sealed in, preserving the full flavour, but there will sometimes be shrinkage. I prefer to slow roast at a lower temperature, a method that will reduce shrinkage and give a more tender joint.

Whichever roasting method you choose, the joint should first be weighed to calculate the cooking time. Place the meat on the grilling rack in the roasting tin, fat side uppermost. This will baste the meat as it is cooking, but check the roast from time to time and using a metal spoon, baste the meat yourself.

If you are using a meat thermometer, do take care when inserting it that it does not touch bone or excess fat. This will give you a false internal reading.

Stuffed joints of meat will need extra cooking time – approximately 10 minutes more for every 500 g (1 lb).

TYPE OF HEAT	TEMPERATURE	TIMING per 500 g (1 lb)
BEEF ON THE BONE SIRLOIN FORE RIB	180°C	RARE 10 mins + 10 mins over MED 12 mins + 12 mins over WELL DONE 20 mins + 20 mins over
BEEF BONED AND ROLLED TOPSIDE TOP RUMP FILLET ROLLED RIB	180°C	RARE 12 mins + 12 mins over MED 15 mins + 15 mins over WELL DONE 20 mins + 20 mins over
PORK ON THE BONE SHOULDER LOIN LEG	180°C	25 mins + 25 mins over
PORK BONED AND ROLLED SHOULDER LOIN LEG	180°C	30 mins + 30 mins over
LAMB ON THE BONE CROWN GUARD OF HONOUR LEG BEST END LOIN	180°C	MED 20 mins + 20 mins over WELL DONE 25 mins + 25 mins over
LAMB BONED AND ROLLED	180°C	MED 25 mins + 25 mins over WELL DONE 30 mins + 30 mins over
VEAL BONED AND ROLLED TOPSIDE SHOULDER FILLET	180°C	MED 20 mins + 20 mins over WELL DONE 25 MINS 25 mins over
VENISON ON THE BONE HAUNCH (LEG) SADDLE	180°C	RARE 12 mins + 12 mins over MED 15 mins + 15 mins over WELL DONE 20 mins + 20 mins over
RABBIT/HARE	180°C	Up to 1 kg (2 lb): 45 – 60 mins Up to 2 kg (4½ lb): 60 – 90 mins
CHICKEN	190°C	20 mins + 20 mins over
TURKEY 3.6–4.5 kg (8–10 lb) 4.9–5.4 kg (11–12 lb) 5.4–6.3 kg (12–14 lb) 6.3–7.2 kg (14–16 lb) 7.2–8.1 kg (16–18 lb) 8.1–9 kg (18–20 lb)	160°C	 3½–3¾ hrs 3¾–4 hrs 4–4¼ hrs 4¼–4½ hrs 4½–4¾ hrs 4¾–5 hrs
DUCK	200°C	MED 25 mins + 25 mins over WELL DONE 30 mins + 30 mins over
GOOSE	180°C	20 mins + 20 mins over
PHEASANT	200°C	50–60 mins total cooking
GROUSE	220°C	30–45 mins total cooking
PARTRIDGE	220°C	45 mins total cooking

RECIPE NOTES
Eggs used are size 3 unless otherwise stated.
All herbs used are fresh unless otherwise stated. If unavailable use dried herbs in half the quantity stated.
Milk should be full-fat unless otherwise stated.
Spoon measures are level unless otherwise stated.

Soups & Starters

Home-made soups are simple to prepare, nutritious and adaptable. Whatever type you are making, you will need a really good stock as the base. There is no mystery attached to the making of a good stock, yet the home stockpot seems to have fallen out of favour. The basic method is the same whether you are making the stock from browned meat bones, a poultry carcass, fish trimmings or vegetables – simply simmer the ingredients in the water until they have yielded their flavours. You may then freeze the stock until required.

Carrot Soup

There is just a hint of orange in this recipe to make it a carrot soup with a difference. Safflower oil is used because it is light in flavour and very low in saturated fat.

25 g (1 oz) butter
1 tablespoon safflower oil
500 g (1 lb) carrots, sliced
1 onion, sliced

1 celery stick, chopped
600 ml (1 pint) vegetable stock (page 19)
2 strips of orange peel

salt and pepper
grated orange zest, to garnish

SERVES 4

METHOD On the hotplate, heat the butter and oil in a saucepan with a lid. Add the vegetables and fry gently for 5–10 minutes.

Add the stock and orange peel and season with salt and pepper. Cover and simmer for 15 minutes or until the vegetables are tender.

Remove the orange peel. Sieve or purée the soup in a blender. The consistency of the soup may be adjusted by adding extra stock if required.

Serve garnished with the grated orange zest.

Chicken Stock

When making chicken stock you can use either raw giblets or a cooked carcass, giblets and pieces of skin.

1 chicken carcass	2 celery sticks, halved	a few parsley stalks
2 onions, quartered	1 teaspoon coarse salt	1.2 litres (2 pints) cold water
2 carrots, halved	6 peppercorns	

MAKES APPROX 900 ML (1½ PINTS)

METHOD Break up the chicken carcass into small sections and place in a large saucepan with a lid. Add all the other ingredients and bring to the boil on the hottest part of the hotplate. Remove any scum and transfer to the coolest part of the hotplate to simmer for 2 hours.

If you are using the main oven the chicken stock may be cooked in a suitable container in the lower oven. If your central heating system is on, utilize the heat transference in the main oven.

Chill the stock until the fat sets in a hard layer on the surface. Using a large metal spoon, lift the solidified fat off carefully and discard. If the stock has to be degreased while still warm, spoon off as much grease as possible using a metal spoon, then float several several thicknesses of kitchen paper across the surface to remove the remaining grease.

This stock can be kept in the refrigerator for 24 hours or frozen for three months.

Vegetable Stock

To make a good vegetable stock you need approximately 1 kg (2 lb) of vegetables to 1.2 litres (2 pints) of water.

1.2 litres (2 pints) water	125 g (4 oz) parsnips, chopped	2–3 cabbage leaves, chopped roughly
4 tablespoons cider vinegar	2 onions, quartered	1 teaspoon salt
250 g (8 oz) carrots, unpeeled, chopped	1 head of celery, sliced roughly	8 peppercorns
250 g (8 oz) leeks, sliced		a few parsley stalks
125 g (4 oz) potatoes, diced		

MAKES APPROX 900 ML (1½ PINTS)

METHOD Place all the ingredients in a large saucepan with a lid and bring to the boil on the hottest part of the hotplate. Skim the surface if necessary and move to the coolest part of the hotplate to simmer for 45 minutes.

Strain through a fine sieve and throw away the vegetables.

This stock can be kept in the refrigerator for 48 hours or frozen for three months.

Brown Stock

To obtain a rich brown stock the bones are first browned in the main oven.

1.25 kg (3 lb) beef marrowbones, cut into pieces
2 onions, quartered

2 carrots, halved
2 celery sticks, halved
1 teaspoon coarse salt
6 peppercorns

a few parsley stalks
2.25–2.75 litres (4–5 pints) cold water

MAKES APPROX 2.25 LITRES (4 PINTS)   **OVEN TEMPERATURE 200°C**

METHOD Preheat the main oven to 200°C. Place the marrowbones in a roasting tin with the vegetables amongst them. Roast in the main oven for 1 hour, basting with the juices half-way through the cooking time.

Transfer the browned bones and vegetables to a large saucepan with a lid. Add the salt, peppercorns, parsley stalks and cold water. Bring to the boil on the hottest part of the hotplate, then remove the scum and slide the saucepan to the coolest part of the hotplate to simmer gently for 3–4 hours.

If you are using the main oven for something else the stock may be cooked in a suitable container in the lower oven. If your central heating system is on, utilize the heat transference in the main oven.

Chill the stock until the fat sets in a hard layer on the surface. Using a large metal spoon, lift the solidified fat off carefully and discard. If the stock has to be degreased while still warm, spoon off as much grease as possible using a metal spoon, then float several thicknesses of kitchen paper across the surface to remove the remaining grease.

This stock can be kept in the refrigerator for 24 hours or frozen for three months.

Fish Stock

1 kg (2 lb) white fish trimmings
1 carrot, chopped roughly
1 onion, chopped roughly

1 handful fresh herbs (parsley, fennel, dill, tarragon)
3 tablespoons lemon juice

10 black pepppercorns
1 litre (1¾ pints) water (a little white wine may be added if preferred)

MAKES ABOUT 750 ML (1¼ PINTS)

METHOD Place the fish trimmings in a large saucepan with the carrot, onion, fresh herbs, lemon juice and peppercorns. Cover with the water, and wine if using. Bring to the boil and simmer for 30 minutes.

Skim the surface to remove scum if necessary and strain the stock. This stock can be kept in the refrigerator for 48 hours or frozen for three months.

Smoked Salmon Baskets

This recipe will suit the cook in a hurry as the filo pastry baskets may be made in advance and the sauce uses a prepared mayonnaise.

2 sheets of filo pastry
50 g (2 oz) butter, melted
75 g (3 oz) smoked salmon pieces

For the cucumber sauce:
½ cucumber, peeled and diced finely
125 ml (4 fl oz) mayonnaise

1 tablespoon lemon juice
salt and pepper
fresh dill, to garnish

SERVES 4

OVEN TEMPERATURE 190°C

METHOD Preheat the main oven to 190°C. To make the filo pastry baskets, grease four ramekin dishes or containers of similar size. Leaving the remaining pastry covered, take 1 sheet of filo pastry and cut in half, then cut each half into quarters, making 8 small squares in all. Brush the pastry squares with melted butter. Place one square in a ramekin. Place a second square crossways over the first and repeat with two more squares. Pinch the corners of the pastry to make them stand up like a flower in the ramekin. Use the remaining four squares to line a second ramekin, then repeat the process with the remaining sheet of filo pastry. Place the ramekins on a baking sheet and bake for 5 minutes until crisp.

To make the cucumber sauce, blend all the ingredients together and chill.

To assemble the baskets, stir the smoked salmon pieces into the chilled sauce. Divide between the baskets just before serving. Garnish with dill.

Pot au Feu

Pot au feu is a traditional French country soup which is allowed to simmer until ready to serve.

600 ml (1 pint) vegetable stock (page 19)
300 ml (½ pint) passata
2 carrots, sliced
2 celery sticks, chopped

2 onions, sliced
½ small white cabbage, sliced
1 leek, sliced
½ small cauliflower, broken into florets

salt and pepper
To garnish:
grated cheese
chopped parsley

SERVES 4

METHOD Place all the ingredients except the garnish in a large saucepan with a lid. Bring to the boil on the hottest part of the hotplate. Cover, remove to the coolest part and simmer gently for 45 minutes.

Serve with the grated cheese and chopped parsley sprinkled on top of the soup.

Pictured over page
Smoked Salmon Baskets
Game Soup, Farmhouse Terrine

Farmhouse Terrine

250 g (8 oz) thin rashers of streaky bacon, de-rinded	*250 g (8 oz) pig's liver, chopped roughly*	*2 tablespoons dry sherry or brandy*
250 g (8 oz) raw chicken, chopped roughly	*25 g (1 oz) butter*	*1 tablespoon chopped mixed herbs*
500 g (1 lb) belly of pork, bones and rind removed	*1 onion, chopped*	*1 egg, beaten*
	2 garlic cloves, crushed	*3 small bay leaves*
	250 g (8 oz) chicken livers, washed and trimmed	*salt and pepper*

SERVES 8 – 10   **OVEN TEMPERATURE 160°C**

METHOD Preheat the main oven to 160°C or cook the terrine in the lower oven if the main oven is being used. Stretch the bacon with a palette knife and line a 1.75-litre (3-pint) terrine dish.

Process the chicken, belly pork and pig's liver in a food processor or blender until roughly chopped.

Melt the butter in a frying-pan on the hotplate and fry the onion and the garlic for a few minutes. Add the chicken livers and fry quickly for 2–3 minutes, then remove the onion, garlic and chicken livers from the pan.

Add the sherry or brandy and the mixed herbs to the pan and stir to deglaze. Add the deglazing liquor to the processed meats along with the beaten egg, season with salt and pepper and mix thoroughly. Place half the mixture in the terrine dish. Add the chicken livers and cover with the remaining mixture. Place the bay leaves on the top and cover the dish with a lid or aluminium foil. Place the dish in a bain-marie and bake for 2 hours.

When cooled, place some weights on top of the foil and leave overnight in the refrigerator. Serve sliced with a green salad and some fresh crusty bread.

Stuffed Mushrooms

Swiss Gruyère cheese gives the sauce a wonderful flavour.

375 (12 oz) cup mushrooms, wiped	*125 g (4 oz) butter, softened*	**For the cheese sauce:**
For the stuffing:	*75 g (3 oz) brown breadcrumbs*	*40 g (1½ oz) butter*
2 garlic cloves, crushed	*125 g (4 oz) bacon rashers, fried or oven-grilled, chopped*	*40 g (1½ oz) plain flour*
2 tablespoons chopped parsley		*450 ml (¾ pint) milk*
a dash of lemon juice		*75 g (3 oz) Gruyère cheese, grated*
		salt and black pepper

SERVES 4–6   **OVEN TEMPERATURE 180°C**

METHOD Preheat the main oven to 180°C. Place the mushrooms in one layer in a shallow ovenproof dish.

To make the stuffing, add the garlic, parsley and lemon juice to the butter and mix well, then add the breadcrumbs. Place a good teaspoonful of the stuffing into each mushroom. Sprinkle the bacon on top of the mushrooms.

To make the cheese sauce, melt the butter in a saucepan on the hotplate. Add the flour and stir until smooth. Cook gently for 2 - 3 minutes, stirring continuously. Remove from the heat and add the milk gradually, stirring after each addition. Return to the heat and bring to the boil, stirring continuously. When the sauce has thickened, add the cheese and season with salt and pepper.

Pour the sauce over the mushrooms and bake in the centre of the oven for 25–30 minutes.

Marinated Mackerel

4 small mackerel fillets	*1 teaspoon pickling spice*	*salt and pepper*
175 ml (6 fl oz) white wine	*2 bay leaves*	***To garnish:***
vinegar	*125 g (4 oz) carrots, cut into*	*frisée leaves*
125 ml (4 fl oz) water	*julienne strips*	*radicchio leaves*
50 g (2 oz) granulated sugar	*1 onion, cut into rings*	

SERVES 4   **OVEN TEMPERATURE 140°C**

METHOD Preheat the main oven to 140°C.

The fishmonger will clean and fillet the mackerel for you but if you prefer to do this yourself, gut and clean the fish, removing the head and tail. Cut open to the back bone from the belly to the tail. Open out slightly and place on a board, cut side down. Beat with a rolling pin along the backbone until the mackerel is flat. Turn it over and pull the backbone away – it will bring most of the bones with it. Check for any remaining bones. Trim off the fins, wash and pat dry with kitchen paper.

Lay the mackerel flat in an ovenproof dish and sprinkle with salt and pepper. Pour the wine vinegar and water over it. Sprinkle with the sugar, pickling spice, bay leaves and vegetables. Cover with aluminium foil and bake in the oven for 1½ hours.

Serve one fillet per person, decorated with the vegetables. Garnish with frisée leaves on one side and radicchio leaves on the other.

Stilton and Walnut Mousse

15 g (½ oz) gelatine
450 ml (¾ pint) cold
  chicken stock (page 19)
250 g (8 oz) Stilton cheese

150 ml (¼ pint) double
  cream
50 g (2 oz) walnuts,
  chopped finely
1 egg white

To decorate:
50 g (2 oz) full fat soft
  cheese
1 tablespoon single cream
walnut halves

SERVES 4–6

METHOD Put the gelatine and 2 tablespoons of the chicken stock in a heatproof bowl and place near the hotplate to dissolve. Heat the remaining stock and add to the dissolved gelatine. Leave to cool.

Cream the Stilton cheese and gradually blend into the stock. Leave in a cool place until just beginning to set.

Whip the cream to a soft consistency and fold into the cheese mixture with the walnuts. Whisk the egg white and fold into the mousse. Spoon carefully into a greased 500 g (1 lb) loaf tin. Cover and leave to set.

Turn the mousse out. To decorate, blend the full fat soft cheese with the cream to a piping consistency. Place in a piping bag fitted with a star nozzle and pipe down the centre of the mousse. Decorate with the walnuts before serving.

Game Soup

A tasty soup based on a stock made from any game bird. Follow the recipe for chicken stock on page 19, substituting a game carcass for the chicken carcass.

1 tablespoon cooking oil
25 g (1 oz) butter
1 onion, chopped
1 leek, chopped

2 large carrots, chopped
2 celery sticks, chopped
1 large potato, chopped
1.2 litres (2 pints) game
  stock

juice of ½ lemon
salt and pepper
chopped parsley, to garnish

SERVES 4

METHOD Heat the butter and oil in a large saucepan on the hotplate. Fry the onions, leek, carrots, celery and potato together for 2–3 minutes. Season with a little salt and pepper, then cover and let the vegetables sweat over low heat for about 15 minutes.

Pour in the game stock and bring slowly to the boil. Add the lemon juice. Allow the soup to simmer gently, covered, on the coolest part of the hotplate for a further 20 minutes until the vegetables are tender. Purée the soup in a blender or food processor.

Check the seasoning and garnish with chopped parsley before serving.

Celtic Niçoise

You can serve this starter hot or, alternatively, cold with a vinaigrette dressing.

4 tablespoons olive oil
750 g (1½ lb) young leeks,
  sliced
175 g (6 oz) tomatoes,
  skinned, de-seeded and
  chopped
1 garlic clove, crushed

1 tablespoon roughly
  chopped tarragon
1 tablespoon lemon juice
zest of 1 lemon
salt and freshly milled black
  pepper

**For the honey and
  mustard vinaigrette:**
1 tablespoon lemon juice
1 teaspoon clear honey
1 teaspoon dried mustard
  powder
3 tablespoons olive oil
salt and black pepper

SERVES 4

METHOD Heat the oil in a frying-pan and add the leeks. Fry gently for 10 minutes or until they are tender. Remove from the pan and keep warm.

Add the tomatoes, garlic and tarragon to the pan, season with salt and pepper and cook gently for 5 minutes.

Add the lemon juice and zest. Return the leeks to the pan and carefully blend all the ingredients together. Serve hot with warm herb bread. Alternatively, chill and serve with the dressing.

To prepare the dressing, put the lemon juice, honey, mustard and salt and pepper into a screw-top jar. Shake well. Add the olive oil and shake again. Chill before using.

Chicken Liver Pâté

250 g (8 oz) butter
250 g (8 oz) chicken livers,
  washed and trimmed
2 garlic cloves, crushed

1 onion, chopped
50 g (2 oz) mushrooms,
  chopped
a pinch of dried thyme

1 tablespoon brandy
2 bay leaves
salt and pepper

SERVES 6

METHOD Melt 175 g (6 oz) butter in a frying-pan on the hotplate and fry the chicken livers for about 3–4 minutes. Add the garlic and onion and cook until the onion is transparent. Add the mushrooms and thyme and fry for a further minute. Take the pan off the heat, add the brandy and season with salt and pepper.

Place the mixture in a food processor or blender and process until smooth. Pour into a 600-ml (1-pint) dish and refrigerate overnight.

To finish the pâté, place the bay leaves on the top, melt the remaining butter and pour over the top of the pâté.

Fish

Fish is a versatile food which is appearing more and more often on our dinner tables in these health-conscious times as it is highly nutritious yet low in saturated fat.
It can be cooked in the most simple fashion – just wrap it in foil or place it in a shallow ovenproof dish with a few vegetables and herbs, cover and bake. The more adventurous cook can delight in grilling, poaching, frying and dressing it up with sauces.

Smoked Haddock Soufflé

This can be cooked in a 1.5-litre (2½-pint) soufflé dish as a main course or in six ramekin dishes as a delicious starter.

15 g (½ oz) butter	*125 g (4 oz) smoked*	*1 teaspoon chopped parsley*
15 g (½ oz) plain flour	*haddock, cooked and*	*4 eggs, separated*
300 ml (½ pint) milk	*flaked*	*salt and pepper*
125 g (4 oz) Lancashire		
cheese, grated		

SERVES 4–6   **OVEN TEMPERATURE 180°C**

METHOD Preheat the main oven to 180°C. Lightly grease the soufflé dish or ramekins with a little butter. Make up a white sauce by placing the butter, flour and milk in a saucepan. Put on the hotplate and whisk continuously until the sauce boils and thickens.

Remove from the heat and add the cheese, smoked haddock, parsley and egg yolks, season with salt and pepper and mix well. Whisk up the egg whites until they reach the soft peak stage and gently fold into the sauce. Pour the mixture into the soufflé dish and bake in the centre of the oven for about 25–30 minutes. If using ramekins, bake towards the top of the oven for 15 minutes.

Baked Grey Mullet

A large fish baked with vegetables makes an inviting whole meal on its own. Grey mullet has firm white flesh that grills and bakes well. It is in season from May to September and will vary in size from 1 kg (2 lb) to 1.5 kg (3½ lb). Vegetables with a high water content help to keep the fish moist.

1 onion, chopped	1.25 kg–1.5 kg (3–3½ lb)	4 tomatoes, skinned, halved
2 tablespoons chopped	grey mullet, cleaned	and de-seeded
parsley	salt and pepper	8 stoned black olives
1 teaspoon chopped	**For the topping:**	4 tablespoons olive oil
marjoram	1 onion, sliced	150 ml (¼ pint) dry white
1 teaspoon chopped oregano	1 green pepper, sliced	wine
2 garlic cloves, chopped	1 red pepper, sliced	

SERVES 4–6 **OVEN TEMPERATURE 150°C**

METHOD Preheat the main oven to 150°C. Grease a gratin dish or line a roasting tin with aluminium foil, depending on the size of the fish. Mix together the onion, herbs and garlic and season with salt and pepper. Place half the mixture in the cleaned fish and half in the prepared dish. Lay the fish on top.

Cover the fish with the sliced vegetables from the topping. Pour the oil and wine over the top. Bake for 30–40 minutes, basting half-way through the cooking time.

Prawn and Mushroom Roulade

75 g (3 oz) soft margarine	**For the filling:**	300 ml (½ pint) milk
75 g (3 oz) plain flour	1 tablespoon oil for frying	125 g (4 oz) prawns, shelled
450 ml (¾ pint) milk	½ onion, chopped	grated zest of 1 lemon
75 g (3 oz) full fat soft	175 g (6 oz) mushrooms,	salt and pepper
cheese	sliced	
3 eggs, separated	50 g (2 oz) soft margarine	
salt and pepper	50 g (2 oz) plain flour	

SERVES 4 **OVEN TEMPERATURE 180°C**

METHOD Preheat the main oven to 180°C. Grease a swiss roll tin measuring 20 × 30 cm (8 × 12 inches). Line with baking parchment.

Melt the margarine in a pan, add the flour and mix well. Remove from the heat. Gradually add the milk and return to the heat to thicken, stirring continuously. Add the cheese and egg yolks, then leave to cool.

Whisk the egg whites and gradually blend into the sauce. Season with salt and pepper and spread the mixture in the prepared tin. Bake for 45 minutes. Remove from the oven. If you are not going to use it immediately, cover with a sheet of greaseproof paper and a damp tea towel.

To make the filling, heat the oil and fry the onions and mushrooms until soft. Add the margarine and melt, stir in the flour and cook for 2 minutes. Blend in the milk. Return to the heat to thicken the sauce, stirring all the time. Add the prawns and lemon zest and season with salt and pepper.

Turn the roulade out on to a sheet of baking parchment and remove the lining paper. Spread the filling evenly and, with the aid of the baking parchment, roll up the roulade.

Mackerel Hotpot

2 tablespoons oil for frying
50 g (2 oz) shallots or small
* onions, chopped*
50 g (2 oz) mushrooms,
* sliced*
3 tablespoons dry white wine

grated zest of 1 lemon
4 mackerel, cleaned
50 g (2 oz) butter
250 g (8 oz) new potatoes,
* boiled and sliced*
2 tomatoes, skinned, de-
* seeded and chopped*

salt and pepper
To garnish:
chopped parsley
grated lemon zest

SERVES 4   **OVEN TEMPERATURE 200°C**

METHOD Preheat the main oven to 200°C. Heat the oil in a frying-pan on the hotplate and gently fry the shallots or small onions and mushrooms until soft. Add the wine and lemon zest, season with salt and pepper and boil briskly to reduce the liquid. Spread the mixture over the base of an ovenproof dish.

Season the inside of the mackerel with salt and pepper and place it on the mushroom mixture.

Heat half the butter in a frying pan and fry the potatoes for 5 minutes. Add the tomatoes and cook for a further 2 minutes.

Cover the fish with the vegetables, dot with the remaining butter and bake for 15 minutes. Serve sprinkled with parsley and lemon zest.

Somerset Casserole

The traditional method for this type of casserole is to thicken the sauce before serving. In order not to disturb the fish, serve it as it is with new potatoes and broccoli for texture.

750 g (1½ lb) fillet of cod or 4 cod steaks, skinned and cubed

2 shallots or small onions, chopped finely
6 tomatoes, skinned, de-seeded and chopped
6 mushrooms, sliced

1 dessert apple, sliced
150 ml (¼ pint) dry cider
50 g (2 oz) butter
salt and pepper

SERVES 4   **OVEN TEMPERATURE 180°C**

METHOD Preheat the main oven to 180°C. Place the fish on a greased ovenproof dish. Cover with the shallots or small onions, tomatoes, mushrooms and apple. Season with salt and pepper and add the cider. Dot with pieces of butter. Cover with aluminium foil and bake for 25 minutes.

Savoury Fish Plait

A family favourite for supper time.

250 g (8 oz) smoked haddock
250 g (8 oz) puff pastry
125 g (4 oz) Cheddar cheese, grated

½ teaspoon grated lemon zest
25 g (1 oz) parsley, chopped
1 egg, hard-boiled and chopped

pepper
1 egg, beaten, to glaze

SERVES 4–6

METHOD Preheat the main oven to 200°C. Poach the fish gently in water for 5–8 minutes. Drain, remove the skin and bones and flake the flesh.

Roll out the pastry on a floured board to a rectangle approximately 30 × 20 cm (12 × 8 inches).

Mix together the fish, cheese, lemon zest, parsley and hard-boiled egg and season with pepper. Place down the centre of the pastry.

Cut the pastry on both sides of the filling at oblique angles 2 cm (¾ inch) apart with a clean, sharp cut. Plait the pastry strips over the filling and brush with egg glaze. Place on a baking sheet and bake for 25 minutes.

Serve hot or cold.

Fish Pie

A lovely, homely fish pie with a 'thatched' potato topping. If you prefer you can omit the smoked haddock and use double the quantity of white fish instead.

375 g (12 oz) smoked haddock
375 g (12 oz) cod or haddock
600 ml (1 pint) milk
1 bay leaf

25 g (1 oz) butter
25 g (1 oz) plain flour
1 tablespoon lemon juice
1 tablespoon chopped parsley
3 eggs, hard-boiled and chopped roughly

2 tomatoes, skinned and sliced
1 kg (2 lb) potatoes, boiled and mashed
salt and freshly milled black pepper

SERVES 6   **OVEN TEMPERATURE 190°C**

METHOD Preheat the main oven to 190C. Poach the fish in the milk with the bay leaf for approximately 15 minutes, either on the coolest part of the hotplate or in the lower oven. When the fish is cooked drain off the milk and reserve. Flake the fish.

Melt the butter in a saucepan on the hotplate. Add the flour and stir until smooth. Cook gently for 2–3 minutes, stirring. Remove from the heat and add the reserved milk gradually, stirring after each addition. Return to the heat and bring to the boil, stirring continuously. When the sauce has thickened add the lemon juice and parsley and season with salt and pepper. Fold in the chopped eggs.

Put the fish into a shallow 1.75-litre (3-pint) ovenproof dish and pour the sauce over it. Arrange the tomatoes on the top.

To make the potato topping, take a forcing bag fitted with a 3 cm (1¼-inch) star nozzle. Fill with the mashed potato and pipe lines across the fish mixture, leaving 2.5 cm (1-inch) gaps. Repeat the process at an angle to create a lattice effect.

Place in the centre of the main oven for 25 minutes until well heated through and lightly brown on top.

Fish Pilaff

Any white fish is suitable for this dish. Coley is dark in appearance when raw, but turns white when cooked.

375 g (12 oz) coley or other white fish
50 g (2 oz) butter
1 onion, chopped finely
½ red pepper, sliced

½ green pepper, sliced
250 g (8 oz) white or brown long-grain rice
½ teaspoon turmeric

600 ml (1 pint) vegetable stock
50 g (2 oz) sultanas
salt and pepper

SERVES 4

METHOD Place the fish in a shallow pan and cover with water. Poach gently for 5–10 minutes. Strain and reserve 150 ml (¼ pint) of the fish liquid.

Melt the butter in a saucepan on the hotplate and fry the onion and peppers until soft. Add the rice and turmeric. Cook for 2–3 minutes, stirring to prevent sticking.

Add the stock and fish liquid, season with salt and pepper and bring to the boil. Move the saucepan to a cooler part of the hotplate and simmer for 12–20 minutes until the rice is tender. (Brown rice will take longer than white to cook and may absorb more liquid.)

Remove the skin and bones from the cooked fish and flake the flesh. Add the fish and sultanas to the rice mixture. Heat through, stirring gently to avoid breaking up the fish. Serve immediately.

Prawn–Stuffed Plaice with Nantua Sauce

Pocket-boning a flat fish for stuffing always produces an impressive dish. Sole or brill could be used as an alternative.

2 *whole plaice*	50 g (2 oz) *mushrooms,*	*For the Nantua sauce:*
For the stuffing:	*chopped*	75 g (3 oz) *butter*
175 g (6 oz) *prawns with*	1 *tablespoon chopped parsley*	20 g (¾ oz) *plain flour*
shells	*grated zest of ½ lemon*	450 ml (¾ pint) *fish stock*
50 g (2 oz) *butter*	*salt and pepper*	*(page 20) or water*
1 *small onion, chopped*		*shells from prawns*
finely		*salt and pepper*

SERVES 2   **OVEN TEMPERATURE 180°C**

METHOD Preheat the main oven to 180°C. Remove the head and gills from the plaice. Trim the fins and remove the dark skin. On the light-skinned side, cut down one side of the backbone, starting 1 cm (½ inch) from the head end. Cut the flesh away, keeping the knife flat to the rib bones. Repeat on the other side to form a pocket.

To remove the backbone, slide the knife in from the head end between the flesh and the backbone to loosen the flesh on the other side. Bend the fish to crack the backbone and, using your fingers, pull the backbone and rib bones away.

To prepare the stuffing, shell the prawns and reserve the shells. Melt the butter in a pan and fry the onion and mushrooms gently until soft. Remove from the heat and add the parsley, lemon zest and prawns. Season with salt and pepper and divide the stuffing between the fish. Place in an ovenproof dish, cover with aluminium foil and bake for 20 minutes.

To make the Nantua sauce, melt 25 g (1 oz) of the butter in a saucepan, add the flour and cook for 2–3 minutes. Gradually add the fish stock or water, whisking constantly as it thickens. Add the reserved prawn shells and simmer for 15 minutes. Strain into a clean saucepan and whisk in the remaining butter. Season with salt and pepper and serve separately.

Poultry & Game

Chicken has become the most popular meat today, as people have increasingly cut back the amount of red meat they eat in the drive to reduce saturated fat in their diets. It is now produced in different forms – corn fed, organic, free range, frozen – to suit all tastes and all pockets. Next to it on the supermarket shelves you are now likely to find game birds, once the preserve of the wealthy, now becoming a favourite dish in many households.

Chicken Ceylon

2 tablespoons groundnut oil
1.5 kg (3½ lb) chicken, jointed
250 g (8 oz) carrots, cut into julienne strips
1 onion, chopped roughly

2 tablespoons curry powder (page 39)
450 ml (¾ pint) chicken stock (page 19)
1 tablespoon tomato purée

50 g (2 oz) creamed coconut, dissolved in 125 ml (4 fl oz) water
250 g (8 oz) cucumber, cut into julienne strips
1 tablespoon chopped coriander leaves

SERVES 4–6

OVEN TEMPERATURE 180°C

METHOD Preheat the main oven to 180°C. Heat the oil in a frying-pan on the hotplate and fry the chicken joints until golden brown. Place in a casserole dish and cover with the carrots.

Fry the onion until soft. Stir in the curry powder and cook for 2 minutes. Remove from the heat and blend in the stock. Return to the heat and bring to the boil to thicken the stock.

Add the tomato purée and creamed coconut to the onion mixture. Pour over the chicken and bake, covered, for 1–1½ hours, until the chicken is tender. Add the coriander leaves, cucumber and salt to taste 15 minutes before the end of the cooking time.

Spicy Chicken

A tasty Saturday treat with an Oriental influence.

4 chicken joints, skinned	*1 tablespoon soya sauce*	*½ teaspoon English mustard*
For the sauce:	*2 teaspoons white vinegar*	*a dash of lemon juice*
1 tablespoon clear honey	*1 teaspoon Worcestershire*	
1 tablespoon apricot jam	*sauce*	

SERVES 4   **OVEN TEMPERATURE 180°C**

METHOD Preheat the main oven to 180°C. Place the chicken joints in a shallow casserole dish.

Mix all the sauce ingredients together in a small saucepan. Heat gently on the simmering plate until well blended. Pour over the chicken joints and cover.

Bake in the centre of the oven for about 20 minutes, then uncover. Return to the oven for a further 20–30 minutes until the sauce is sticky and the chicken is cooked.

Evesham Turkey

An easy and attractive way to serve turkey in an unusual fruity sauce.

1 turkey breast, skinned and cut into 1 cm (½-inch) strips (goujons)	*1 teaspoon chopped parsley*	*250 g (8 oz) plums, stoned and quartered*
1 teaspoon chopped thyme	*250 g (8 oz) patna rice, boiled*
150 ml (¼ pint) white grape juice	*a dash of Worcestershire sauce*	*salt and pepper*
½ onion, chopped very finely	*oil for frying*	
	25 g (1 oz) butter	

SERVES 4

METHOD Place the strips of turkey in a shallow dish and pour the grape juice over them. Add the onion, herbs and Worcestershire sauce and cover. Place in the refrigerator to marinate for at least 4 hours.

Remove the turkey from the marinade and drain. Melt the oil and butter in a large frying-pan on the hotplate, add the turkey and fry until lightly browned. Add the marinade and plums and season with salt and pepper. Cover the pan, move it to the coolest part of the hotplate and allow to simmer gently for 15–20 minutes. Serve on a bed of boiled rice.

Stir-Fried Chicken with Pancakes

2 chicken breasts, boned and
  skinned
1 tablespoon cornflour
2 teaspoons Chinese 5-spice
  powder
1 tablespoon safflower oil
1 teaspoon sesame oil

1 garlic clove, chopped
125 g (4 oz) bean sprouts
1 green pepper, sliced
125 ml (4 fl oz) chicken
  stock (page 19)
1 tablespoon dark soya sauce
¼ cucumber, cut into strips

For the pancake batter:
125 g (4 oz) plain flour
a pinch of salt
1 egg, beaten
300 ml (½ pint) milk
oil for frying

SERVES 4

METHOD To prepare the pancake batter, sift the flour and salt into a large bowl. Make a hollow in the centre of the flour and drop in the beaten egg. Pour half the milk into the flour, gradually working the flour into the milk.

When all the flour is incorporated beat the mixture (if using a food processor take care not to over-beat or you will 'toughen' the batter).

Add the remaining milk. The batter should have the consistency of single cream.

Lightly oil a crêpe pan and heat on the hotplate. Pour in just enough batter to make the size of pancake required (1 tablespoon of batter makes a neat pancake for serving with this recipe). Cook the pancake for 1 minute on each side. Cover and keep warm while you make the remaining pancakes, either near the hotplate or in the lower oven.

To prepare the stir-fried chicken, slice the chicken breasts into thin strips. Mix together the cornflour and Chinese 5-spice powder and toss with the chicken pieces to coat them evenly.

Heat the oils in a wok or heavy-based frying pan. Stir-fry the chicken for 3 minutes or until cooked, remove to a plate and keep warm near the hotplate.

Add the garlic, bean sprouts and green pepper and stir-fry for 2 minutes. Add the stock, soya sauce and cucumber and heat through, stirring continuously. Return the chicken to the pan and stir well until it is heated through. Fold the pancakes into quarters and serve with the stir-fry.

Curry Powder

1 tablespoon ground
  coriander
1 teaspoon ground cumin

1 teaspoon turmeric
½ teaspoon chilli powder
½ teaspoon ground ginger

¼ teaspoon ground cinnamon
¼ teaspoon freshly milled
  black pepper

SERVES 6

METHOD Mix all the ingredients together.

Poacher's Pie

1 tablespoon flour
1 teaspoon dried mustard
    powder
1.25 kg (3 lb) rabbit,
    jointed
2 tablespoons oil for frying

250 g (8 oz) streaky bacon,
    chopped
250 g (8 oz) sausagemeat
1 tablespoon chopped parsley
1 teaspoon chopped sage
2 leeks, sliced thinly
2 carrots, sliced thinly

125 g (4 oz) button
    mushrooms
300 ml (½ pint) vegetable
    stock (page 19)
500 g (1 lb) potatoes, boiled
    and sliced
salt and pepper

SERVES 4 **OVEN TEMPERATURE 180°C**

METHOD Preheat the main oven to 180°C. Season the flour with salt, pepper and mustard. Coat the rabbit joints completely with the seasoned flour.

Heat the oil in a frying-pan, add the bacon and cook slowly until lightly browned.

Mix the sausagemeat and herbs together, form into balls and add to the frying-pan. Fry until golden. Remove the bacon and sausagemeat from the frying-pan and keep warm on the hotplate. Fry the rabbit joints, 2 at a time, until lightly coloured.

Layer the rabbit joints, bacon, sausagemeat balls, leeks, carrots and mushrooms in a casserole dish. Pour in the vegetable stock and top with overlapping potato slices. Cover and cook for 20 minutes in the oven, then uncover and cook for a further 15 minutes.

Chicken Archduke

2 tablespoons safflower oil
1.5 kg (3½ lb) chicken,
    jointed
1 garlic clove, crushed
1 onion, chopped
40 g (1½ oz) plain flour

350 ml (12 fl oz) chicken
    stock (page 19)
4 tablespoons dry sherry
1 cucumber, peeled and cut
    into chunks
50 g (2 oz) button
    mushrooms

150 ml (¼ pint) carton
    soured cream
salt and pepper
To garnish:
chopped parsley
cucumber slices

SERVES 4–6

METHOD Heat the oil in a frying-pan on the hotplate and lightly fry the chicken joints without colouring them. Remove from the pan and keep warm (the insulating lid on the hotplate is ideal for this).

Add the garlic and onion to the pan and fry until soft. Add the flour and cook without browning for 2–3 minutes. Remove from the heat and slowly blend in the chicken stock. Return to the heat to thicken the sauce.

Add the sherry and chicken and season with salt and pepper. Cover and simmer gently for 30 minutes. Add the cucumber and mushrooms and cook for a further 15 minutes.

Stir in the soured cream and serve garnished with parsley and cucumber slices.

Oven–Baked Chicken with Avocado Sauce

An ideal recipe for a buffet party, with an attractive sauce.

2 tablespoons oil for frying
1 egg, beaten
125 g (4 oz) fresh
*   breadcrumbs*
50 g (2 oz) almonds,
*   chopped finely*

8 chicken drumsticks,
*   skinned*
salt and pepper
For the avocado sauce:
1 large avocado pear
zest and juice of 1 lemon

150 ml (¼ pint) greek-style
*   yogurt*
½ garlic clove, crushed
salt and pepper

SERVES 4	OVEN TEMPERATURE 190°C

METHOD Preheat the main oven to 190°C. In a bowl, mix together the oil and egg and season with salt and pepper. Place the breadcrumbs and almonds on a sheet of greaseproof paper. Dip the chicken drumsticks into the egg mixture, then coat with the breadcrumbs and nuts.

Place the drumsticks on a greased baking sheet 5 cm (2 inches) apart. Cover with aluminium foil and bake for 30 minutes. Remove the aluminium and cook for a further 20 minutes or until the chicken is tender.

To make the avocado sauce, scrape the avocado flesh into a bowl, making sure you remove the flesh from near the skin to give the sauce a good colour. Mix all the ingredients together to form a pale green purée. Cover tightly to prevent discolouration and chill. Use the same day.

Roast Duckling with Gooseberry Sauce

1.75–2.25 kg (4 lb–5 lb)
*   duckling*
For the stuffing:
heart and liver of the duck,
*   chopped finely*
50 g (2 oz) butter

125 g (4 oz) fresh
*   breadcrumbs*
250 g (8 oz) gooseberries,
*   halved*
zest and juice of ½ orange
1 egg, beaten

salt and pepper
For the gooseberry sauce:
250 g (8 oz) gooseberries
zest and juice of ½ orange
50 g (2 oz) granulated sugar

SERVES 4	OVEN TEMPERATURE 200°C

METHOD Preheat the main oven to 200°C. To make the stuffing, fry the chopped giblets in the melted butter until they turn grey.

In a bowl, mix together the breadcrumbs, gooseberries and orange zest and juice. Season with salt and pepper and stir in the giblets. Bind together with the egg and use to stuff the duckling.

Prick the duckling all over with a skewer or a sharp fork and sprinkle with salt. This helps to draw out the fat and crisp the skin. Place the duckling on the grilling rack in a roasting tin and place in the oven. See the chart on page 17 for roasting times.

To make the gooseberry sauce, simmer the gooseberries in 2 tablespoons water and the orange juice until tender.

Pass the gooseberries through a sieve and return the purée to the saucepan. Add the orange zest and sugar and stir over a gentle heat to dissolve the sugar. Serve the sauce separately.

Braised Pheasant

Apricots and other dried fruits lend themselves very well to game dishes. The age of the pheasant will determine the length of cooking time; allow an extra 1–2 hours for an older bird. To make game stock, follow the recipe for chicken stock on page 19, substituting a game carcass for the chicken.

25 g (1 oz) butter	*300 ml (½ pint) dry white wine*	*a little cornflour to thicken the juices*
2 tablespoons oil for frying		
1 large pheasant or a brace of smaller birds	*300 ml (½ pint) game stock*	*250 g (8 oz) button mushrooms*
1 small onion, sliced	*1 bay leaf*	
1 carrot, sliced	*1 teaspoon chopped thyme*	*142 ml (¼ pint) carton of single cream*
125 g (4 oz) dried no-soak apricots	*250 g (8 oz) shallots or small onions*	*salt and black pepper*

SERVES 4–6   **OVEN TEMPERATURE 150°C**

METHOD Preheat the main oven to 150°C. Heat the butter and oil in a large casserole on the hotplate. Add the pheasant and fry quickly until brown. Remove from the casserole and place on a plate.

Add the onion and the carrot to the casserole and fry gently for 1 minute. Stir in the apricots, white wine and stock and flavour with the bay leaf, chopped thyme and salt and pepper.

Return the pheasant to the casserole. Cover and bring to the boil, then allow to simmer for 15 minutes on the coolest part of the hotplate.

Stir in the shallots or small onions and transfer to the main oven. Cook for 4–5 hours, or until the pheasant is tender.

Lift the pheasant out of the casserole, take the meat off the bone and place on one side. Remove the bay leaf from the casserole. Mix the cornflour with a little water and add to the casserole. Allow to thicken on the hotplate. Add the mushrooms.

Return the pheasant meat to the sauce and finally pour in the cream to finish (do not allow to boil). Serve with mashed potatoes and seasonal vegetables.

Meat

Different methods of cooking suit different cuts of meat, and hitting upon the right combination will bring out the very best flavours and textures. The recipes here give a range of dishes that are guaranteed to please – but go on to experiment with other cuts, season them with herbs and spices and serve them with tender vegetables cooked al dente. Your Stanley cooker will deal equally well with a rare beef roast and a casserole of a cheaper meat cooked long and slow.

Casserole of Kidneys in Red Wine

6–8 lamb's kidneys, skinned and cored
250 g (8 oz) chipolata sausages
50 g (2 oz) butter

2 onions, sliced
1 tablespoon plain flour
450 ml (¾ pint) brown stock (page 20)
150 ml (¼ pint) red wine

2 tablespoons tomato purée
250 g (8 oz) mushrooms, sliced
salt and black pepper

SERVES 4–6　　　　　　　　　　　　　　　**OVEN TEMPERATURE 160°C**

METHOD Preheat the main oven to 160°C. Place the kidneys and sausages with the butter in a casserole and fry until brown on all sides. Lift out on to a plate. Add the onions and fry until soft.

Add the flour and cook for a few moments. Slowly blend in the stock and the wine, stirring until the sauce reaches the boil.

Add the tomato purée and season with salt and pepper. Replace the kidneys and sausages. Add the mushrooms. Cover and place in the main oven for about 20–30 minutes.

Creamed Pork with Prunes

250 g (8 oz) prunes, stoned
150 ml (¼ pint) dry white
* wine*

1 tenderloin of pork (fillet),
* cut into slices*
50 g (2 oz) plain flour,
* seasoned*

50 g (2 oz) butter
1 tablespoon oil for frying
300 ml (½ pint) double
* cream*

SERVES 4   **OVEN TEMPERATURE 150°C**

METHOD Preheat the main oven to 150°C. (The lower oven could be used, depending on what mode you are operating your cooker on.)

Poach the prunes in the wine in a covered dish for 1 hour. Strain and reserve the liquid.

Coat the pork slices with the seasoned flour. Heat the butter and oil in a frying-pan and fry the pork for 5 minutes until it is golden brown on both sides.

Place the pork on a warmed serving dish and arrange the prunes around it. Keep warm. Pour the liquid from the prunes into the frying-pan. Stir to deglaze and reduce the liquid, using the hottest part of the hotplate.

Add the cream, remove the frying-pan from the heat and stir gently. Pour the sauce over the pork and serve hot.

Tenderloin of Pork in Orange Marinade

This cut of pork is often split and stuffed before roasting. This recipe leaves it whole but uses an orange-flavoured marinade prior to roasting. A 'dry' marinade is smeared on to the meat to keep this lean cut moist.

1 tenderloin of pork (fillet)
For the marinade:
grated zest of 1 orange

1 tablespoon safflower oil
1 garlic clove, crushed
½ teaspoon dried mustard
* powder*

1 tablespoon chopped sage
1 teaspoon ground ginger

SERVES 4–6   **OVEN TEMPERATURE 190°C**

METHOD To prepare the marinade, mix all the ingredients together in a shallow dish. Roll the tenderloin of pork in the marinade and leave in the refrigerator for at least 2 hours.

Preheat the main oven to 190°C. Lay the tenderloin in a lightly greased roasting tin and roast according to the chart on page 17.

Serve with Fan-Shaped Roast Potatoes (page 92).

Crown Roast of Lamb

A spectacular roast to serve for a special occasion. If you are short of time most butchers will make the crown of lamb for you if given advance notice.

2 best ends of neck of lamb, chined
For the celery and walnut stuffing:
25 g (1 oz) butter
1 onion, chopped finely

4 celery sticks, chopped finely
125 g (4 oz) fresh breadcrumbs
50 g (2 oz) walnuts, chopped
grated zest and juice of orange

1 tablespoon chopped parsley
salt and black pepper
To garnish:
parsley sprigs
cutlet frills

SERVES 6–8   **OVEN TEMPERATURE 180°C**

METHOD Preheat the main oven to 180°C. To prepare the crown roast, trim the fat and skin from the ends of the rib bones so that 2 cm (¾ inch) of the bone is displayed. Place the joints back to back and sew the ends together, using a trussing needle and string, to form a crown shape.

To prepare the stuffing, melt the butter in a saucepan on the hotplate and lightly fry the onion. Remove from the heat and mix in the remaining ingredients.

Place the crown of lamb in a roasting tin and put the stuffing in the centre. Cover the top of the crown of lamb with aluminium foil to keep the stuffing moist and to prevent the bones from burning during cooking. Roast in the centre of the oven (see the chart on page 17 for roasting times).

Remove the aluminium foil when the lamb is cooked. Garnish the roast with parsley and place a cutlet frill on each bone.

Crown Roast of Lamb

Lamb Burgers

A tasty treat for children or adults that requires very little preparation.

500 g (1 lb) leg or shoulder of lamb, minced

50 g (2 oz) cooked apple, grated

1 tablespoon chopped mint

SERVES 4–6	OVEN TEMPERATURE 190°C

METHOD Mix all the ingredients together thoroughly. Divide the mixture into 4 large or 6 small portions. Flour or wet your hands and form into burger shapes. Chill before cooking.

TO COOK ON THE HOTPLATE: Set the cooker to the hotplate mode. Brush the hotplate with a little oil and cook the lamb burgers for 3 minutes on each side for rare, 5 minutes on each side for medium.

TO COOK IN THE OVEN: Preheat the oven to 190°C. Place the burgers in a roasting tin and bake for 15–20 minutes. Cooking in the oven draws more fat out of the lamb so this is a healthier way than cooking on the hotplate, but not as appealing to the eye. Try serving oven-baked burgers in the pocket of white or wholemeal pitta bread.

Beef Olives

There are numerous variations on the base of this stuffing. This recipe uses sausagemeat.

250 g (8 oz) topside of beef
125 g (4 oz) beef sausagemeat
2 teaspoons chopped parsley
1 tablespoon oil for frying

25 g (1 oz) butter
25 g (1 oz) plain flour
300 ml (½ pint) brown stock (page 20)
125 g (4 oz) celery, chopped

250 g (8 oz) carrots, sliced thinly
1 bouquet garni
salt and pepper

SERVES 3–4	OVEN TEMPERATURE 190°C

METHOD Preheat the main oven to 190°C. Cut the meat into small, thin slices. Beat with a meat hammer or rolling pin to break down the fibres.

Mix together the sausagemeat and parsley. Spread a small amount on each piece of meat and roll up. Tie with string.

Melt the oil and butter in a frying-pan and seal the beef olives. Transfer to a casserole dish.

Blend the flour into the fat and cook for 2–3 minutes. Remove from the heat and stir in the stock. Return to the heat and stir until thickened.

Add the vegetables, bouquet garni and salt and pepper. Pour the mixture over the beef olives. Cover and cook for 1½ hours. The water content of the celery dilutes the sauce during cooking.

Sautéed Liver with Lemon

The speed of cooking in this recipe prevents the liver from becoming tough.

75 g (3 oz) plain flour
500 g (1 lb) lamb's liver,
*   sliced thinly*

50 g (2 oz) butter
2 onions, sliced
zest and juice of ½ lemon

salt and pepper
1–2 tablespoons chopped
*   parsley, to garnish*

SERVES 4

METHOD   Season the flour with salt and pepper. Roll the liver in the flour until it is coated.

Melt the butter in a large frying-pan on the hotplate, add the onions and fry until soft. Add the lemon zest and the liver and fry quickly on both sides until the liver is cooked. Add the lemon juice to flavour and garnish with the chopped parsley.

Oxtail Casserole

Oxtail is a very underrated cut of meat which lends itself to long, slow cooking to make this wholesome casserole. There is no need to add any extra fat for frying as the oxtail has sufficient.

1.1–1.25 kg (2½–3 lb)
*   oxtail, cut into pieces and*
*   trimmed*
2 onions, sliced
2 large carrots, sliced

2 celery sticks, sliced
2 parsnips, cut into pieces
25–50 g (1–2 oz) plain
*   flour*
425 g (14 oz) can of
*   chopped tomatoes*

600 ml (1 pint) brown stock
*   (page 20)*
2 bay leaves
1 teaspoon dried mixed herbs
salt and black pepper

SERVES 6   **OVEN TEMPERATURE 150°C**

METHOD   Preheat the main oven to 150°C. Fry the oxtail in a frying-pan on the hotplate until brown. Place in a casserole.

Fry the onions in the pan for about 2 minutes. Add the carrots, celery and parsnips and cook for about 5 minutes.

Add the flour and mix well. Add the tomatoes, stock, bay leaves and herbs, season with salt and pepper and stir until the sauce begins to thicken. Pour over the oxtail. Transfer to the coolest part of the hotplate. Cover and allow to simmer gently for 10 minutes.

Transfer to the main oven for about 4–5 hours or until the oxtail is tender. Allow the casserole to go cold. Skim off any surplus fat. Reheat and check the seasoning. Serve with mashed potatoes.

Pictured over page
Sautéed Liver with Lemon
Oxtail Casserole, Harvest Pork

Harvest Pork

This sweet sauce can also be served with lamb chops.

4 pork chops (loin or
  chump), trimmed
25 g (1 oz) butter
1 onion, chopped
1 garlic clove, crushed
1 red-skinned dessert apple,
  chopped

50 g (2 oz) raisins
½ teaspoon ground ginger
pinch of dried mustard
  powder
1 tablespoon clear honey
300 ml (½ pint) brown
  stock (page 20)

25 g (1 oz) cornflour
salt and pepper
To garnish:
1 red-skinned dessert apple,
  sliced
chopped parsley

SERVES 4　　　　　　　　　　　　　　　　**OVEN TEMPERATURE 200°C**

METHOD　Preheat the main oven to 200°C. Place the chops on the grilling grid in a roasting tin and cook on a high shelf in the oven for 20 minutes. This will remove any excess fat from the chops.

Meanwhile, melt the butter in a saucepan on the hotplate and gently fry the onion and garlic until softened. Add the apple, raisins, ginger, mustard, honey and most of the stock. Simmer gently for 3–5 minutes.

With the remaining stock, mix the cornflour to a paste and use to thicken the sauce. Season with salt and pepper.

Remove the chops from the oven and place in a casserole dish. Pour the sauce over the chops. Cover and cook for 30 minutes or until the chops are tender.

Serve the chops in the casserole dish, garnished with apple and parsley.

Lamb Pies

250 g (8 oz) hot water crust
  pastry (page 65)
1 egg, beaten, to glaze
For the filling:
1 tablespoon oil for frying
25 g (1 oz) butter

1 onion, chopped
1 garlic clove, crushed
375 g (12 oz) lamb leg
  fillet, cubed
125 g (4 oz) carrots,
  chopped finely

300 ml (½ pint) brown
  stock (page 20)
25 g (1 oz) cornflour
1 tablespoon tomato purée
salt and pepper

SERVES 4–6　　　　　　　　　　　　**OVEN TEMPERATURE 180° & 200°C**

METHOD　Preheat the main oven to 180°C. To prepare the filling, heat the oil and butter in a frying-pan and fry the onion and garlic until soft. Add the cubed lamb and cook until browned. Transfer to a casserole dish. Add the carrots and stock and season to taste with salt and pepper. Cook in the oven for 2 hours.

Combine the cornflour with a little cold water and mix to a paste. Add the tomato purée and cornflour to the casserole and cook until thickened. Allow to cool completely before using to make the pies.

To make the pies, preheat the oven to 200°C. While the pastry is still warm, use two-thirds of it to line greased ramekin dishes for individual pies or an 18 cm (7-inch) spring-clip tin.

Fill to the top with the cold lamb mixture. Press the remaining pastry out with floured hands to form lids. Cover the pies with the remaining pastry and use a fork to decorate and to seal the edges of the pies.

Decorate with pastry trimmings and brush with a little beaten egg. Bake for 30–35 minutes until golden brown. The individual pies will easily slide out of the ramekin dishes when either hot or cold.

Royal Guard of Honour

This rack of lamb is served cold with an unusual stuffing.

	For the stuffing:	For the dressing:
2 matching best ends of neck of lamb	175 g (6 oz) white cabbage, shredded finely	3 tablespoons walnut oil
1 teaspoon dried mustard powder	175 g (6 oz) red cabbage, shredded finely	1 tablespoon white wine vinegar
salt and pepper	4 celery sticks, chopped	1 teaspoon coarse-grain mustard
	25 g (1 oz) walnuts, chopped roughly	½ teaspoon caraway seeds
		salt and pepper

SERVES 6   **OVEN TEMPERATURE 180°C**

METHOD Preheat the main oven to 180°C. To prepare the lamb, remove the chine bones. Carefully remove the skin from the fat. Using a sharp knife, remove 8 cm (3 inches) of fat and flesh from the end of the rib bones. Scrape the bones clean.

Stand the racks upright and interlink the rib bones with the fat outermost. Tie together and score the fat with a criss-cross pattern. Mix together the mustard, salt and pepper and rub into the fat. Cover the ends of the rib bones with aluminium foil to prevent them from burning. Roast in the centre of the oven (see the chart on page 17 for roasting times). Remove from the oven and leave to cool.

To prepare the stuffing, mix all the ingredients together in a large bowl.

To prepare the dressing, blend the oil and vinegar together then add the mustard, caraway seeds and salt and pepper.

To assemble the Royal Guard of Honour, place the cold rack of lamb on a serving platter. Blend the dressing and the stuffing together and place in the rack of lamb. Decorate with cutlet frills.

Country Casserole

A traditional casserole with herb-flavoured dumplings.

2 tablespoons oil for frying
500 g (1 lb) braising steak
25 g (1 oz) butter
1 onion, chopped
2 leeks, sliced
2 carrots, sliced

300 ml (½ pint) brown
  stock (page 20)
50 g (2 oz) green lentils,
  picked over, washed and
  drained
salt and pepper

For the dumplings:
125 g (4 oz) self-raising
  flour
50 g (2 oz) suet
1 tablespoon chopped parsley
1 teaspoon dried mixed herbs
100 ml (3½ oz) water

SERVES 4　　　　　　　　　**OVEN TEMPERATURE 180°C**

METHOD Preheat the main oven to 180°C. Heat the oil in a frying-pan on the hotplate. Fry the meat quickly to seal and brown it. Transfer to a casserole dish.

Add the butter to the frying-pan and lightly fry the vegetables. Add to the meat.

Stir in the stock and lentils. Season with salt and pepper. Cover and cook for 1 hour.

To prepare the dumplings, put all the dry ingredients into a bowl and mix with the water to a soft dough. Flour your hands and shape into small dumplings.

Place the dumplings on top of the meat and return the casserole to the oven, uncovered, for 30 minutes.

Hawich Beef

1 tablespoon oil for frying
1 kg (2 lb) shin of beef,
  trimmed and cubed
1½ tablespoons plain flour
1 teaspoon curry powder
  (page 39)

2 onions, sliced
2 garlic cloves, crushed
4–6 celery sticks, chopped
425 (14 oz) can of chopped
  tomatoes
2 teaspoons tomato purée

150 ml (¼ pint) red wine
450 ml (¾ pint) brown
  stock (page 20)
175 g (6 oz) button
  mushrooms
salt and pepper

SERVES 6　　　　　　　　　**OVEN TEMPERATURE 150°C**

METHOD Preheat the main oven to 150°C. Heat the oil in a large casserole on the hotplate. Add the beef and fry quickly to seal in the juices and brown the meat. Stir in the flour and curry powder and fry for 1 minute. Add the onions and garlic and fry until soft.

Add the remaining ingredients except the mushrooms and gradually bring to the boil. Cover and simmer gently on the coolest part of the hotplate for 10–15 minutes. Transfer to the main oven for about 4–5 hours until the meat is tender. Check the seasoning and stir in the mushrooms 5 minutes before the end of the cooking time.

Vegetable Dishes

For too long in this country we regarded our vegetables as just an accompaniment to meat. Now that we have the chance, through travel and through television programmes, to see how vegetables are used in other countries we are beginning to accord them the respect they truly deserve. Today, we are finally realising what vegetarians have always known – that a vegetable dish can be exciting in flavour and texture as well as being a healthier alternative to meat.

Sautéed Brussels Sprouts

500 g (1 lb) brussels sprouts
1 tablespoon oil for frying
1 green pepper, sliced finely,
  1 onion, chopped

375 g (12 oz) tomatoes,
  skinned, de-seeded and
  chopped

1 teaspoon chopped basil
salt and freshly milled black
  pepper

SERVES 4

METHOD Trim the sprouts and make a cut in the base of each. Cook in boiling salted water for 5 minutes. Drain.

Heat the oil in a sauté pan and cook the onion and pepper until soft.

Add the sprouts, tomatoes, basil and seasoning and heat through. Serve immediately.

Potato Bake

This is an excellent dish as it does not spoil if your guests are delayed or the family are late home from work. It is ideal served with oven-baked chops or roast lamb, pork or ham.

1 kg (2 lb) potatoes, sliced thinly *2 onions, sliced*	*1 tablespoon snipped chives* *300 ml (½ pint) milk*	*75 g (3 oz) Cheddar cheese, grated* *salt and pepper*

SERVES 4–6	**OVEN TEMPERATURE 180°C**

METHOD Preheat the main oven to 180°C. Layer the sliced potatoes, onions and chives into a 1.5-litre (2½-pint) shallow ovenproof dish.

Heat the milk in a small saucepan on the hotplate and season well. Pour the milk over the vegetables. Cover with a lid or a piece of foil. Bake in the centre of the oven for about 45 minutes.

Remove the dish from the oven, uncover and sprinkle the cheese on the top. Return the dish to the oven and cook until golden-brown and the milk has been absorbed by the potatoes, approximately 25 minutes.

Place the cooked dish in the lower oven until ready to serve.

Mange Tout, Celery and Sweetcorn in Herb Butter

This dish is quick and easy to prepare. Serve as an accompaniment to lamb, ham or chicken.

75 g (3 oz) butter *1 small head of celery, chopped*	*250 g (8 oz) mange tout* *125 g (4 oz) sweetcorn* *2 tablespoons chopped parsley*	*1 tablespoon chopped chives* *salt and pepper*

SERVES 6

METHOD Place a large frying-pan on the hotplate and melt the butter. Add the celery and mange tout and stir-fry for about 3 minutes. Add the sweetcorn, parsley and chives. Season with salt and pepper and stir-fry for a further 2 minutes.

Pictured over page: *Potato Bake*
Mangetout, Celery and Sweetcorn in Herb Butter
Herby Nut Roast

Herby Nut Roast

1 tablespoon oil for frying	250 g (8 oz) mixed nuts,	250 g (8 oz) tomatoes,
1 onion, chopped	chopped	skinned, de-seeded and
½ green pepper, sliced thinly	75 g (3 oz) fresh white or	chopped
½ red pepper, sliced thinly	brown breadcrumbs	1 egg, beaten
1 celery stick, chopped	1 garlic clove, crushed	salt and pepper
	1 tablespoon chopped parsley	
	1 teaspoon chopped tarragon	
	1 teaspoon pesto sauce	

SERVES 4 **OVEN TEMPERATURE 220°C**

METHOD Preheat the main oven to 220°C. Heat the oil in a frying-pan and fry the onion, peppers and celery until soft.

In a large bowl, mix together the nuts, breadcrumbs, garlic, herbs and pesto sauce. Stir in the tomatoes and cooked vegetables. Bind with beaten egg and season with salt and pepper.

Press firmly into a greased 18 cm (7 inch) square tin and bake in the oven for 30–40 minutes. Serve hot or cold with a salad.

Cabbage Pie

Children who will not normally eat cabbage will adore the cheesy flavour of this pie.

250 g (8 oz) shortcrust	½ white cabbage, shredded	salt and pepper
pastry or nut-flavoured	1 cooking apple, grated	1 egg, beaten, to glaze
pastry (page 69)	250 g (8 oz) Cheddar	
50 g (2 oz) butter	cheese, grated	

SERVES 4 **OVEN TEMPERATURE 200°C**

METHOD Preheat the main oven to 200°C. Roll out two-thirds of the pastry on a floured board and use it to line a greased 900 ml (1½–pint) pie dish.

Melt the butter in a deep saucepan and fry the cabbage gently for 5 minutes. Keep stirring to prevent the cabbage from browning.

Fill the pie dish with layers of cabbage, grated apple and cheese, seasoning each layer lightly with salt and pepper.

Roll out the remaining pastry to form a lid. Wet the rim of the pastry shell to help it seal. Lift it over the pie dish and trim off the excess pastry. Knock back the edges to seal and crimp. Decorate with pastry trimmings. Brush with egg glaze and bake for 25–30 minutes.

Savoury Stuffed Cabbage Leaves

This can be turned into a vegetarian recipe by substituting basmati rice, nuts and dried fruits for the meat.

8 large cabbage leaves	125 g (4 oz) carrot, grated	250 ml (8 fl oz) passata or
1 tablespoon oil for frying	125 g (4 oz) mushrooms,	vegetable stock (page 19)
1 onion, chopped	chopped	salt and pepper
375 g (12 oz) minced beef	2 tomatoes, chopped	
or lamb	1 teaspoon pesto sauce	

SERVES 4 **OVEN TEMPERATURE 180°C**

METHOD Preheat the main oven to 180°C. Remove the hard stalk from the base of each cabbage leaf using a V-shaped cut. Blanch the leaves in boiling salted water for 3 minutes. Drain and wrap in kitchen paper.

Heat the oil in a frying-pan, add the onion and fry until soft. Add the minced beef or lamb and cook for 5 minutes, stirring occasionally. Add the carrots, mushrooms, tomatoes, pesto sauce and salt and pepper. Cook gently for 5 minutes.

Divide the filling between the cabbage leaves. Fold in the outer edges of the leaves to neaten, then roll up to enclose the filling completely. Place the cabbage leaf parcels in a shallow ovenproof dish and pour passata or vegetable stock over them. Cover and bake for 45 minutes.

Vegetable Goulash

During the winter months this recipe can be changed to a cobbler, using root vegetables with a cheese scone topping; omit the soured cream.

2 tablespoons groundnut oil	4 tomatoes, skinned, de-	1 tablespoon chopped basil
2 onions, chopped	seeded and chopped	150 ml (¼ pint) carton
1 tablespoon paprika	2 celery sticks, chopped	soured cream
150 ml (¼ pint) passata	1 kg (2 lb) assorted	**To garnish:**
150 ml (¼ pint) vegetable	vegetables, cut into chunks	1 teaspoon paprika
stock (page 19)	a pinch of salt	freshly milled black pepper

SERVES 4 **OVEN TEMPERATURE 180°C**

METHOD Preheat the main oven to 180°C. Heat the oil in an ovenproof dish and fry the onions with the paprika until soft.

Add the passata and vegetable stock, bring to the boil and stir in the vegetables, salt and basil. Cover and bake for 30–40 minutes, depending on the vegetables used.
Stir in the soured cream and garnish with black pepper and paprika.

Courgette and Cheese Bake

A delicious lunch or supper dish, and an imaginative way to use up a glut of courgettes in the summer.

25 g (1 oz) butter or
  margarine
1 onion, chopped
1 garlic clove, crushed
500 g (1 lb) courgettes,
  grated

175 g (6 oz) brown
  breadcrumbs
125 g (4 oz) Cheddar
  cheese, grated
250 g (8 oz) fromage frais
300 ml (½ pint) milk

2 eggs, beaten
1 teaspoon chopped parsley
1 teaspoon English mustard
salt and pepper

SERVES 4   **OVEN TEMPERATURE 190°C**

METHOD Preheat the main oven to 190°C. Lightly butter a 1.5-litre (2½- pint) ovenproof dish. Melt the butter or margarine in a large saucepan and fry the onion and garlic until soft. Add the courgettes and fry gently for 2 minutes. Add all the remaining ingredients and mix well.

Pour into the ovenproof dish and bake in the centre of the oven for 45 minutes.

Cheese and Mushroom Omelette

Use a heavy-based omelette pan to make this light and fluffy omelette.

1 tablespoon olive oil
2 eggs

50 g (2 oz) Double
  Gloucester cheese with
  chives, grated

50 g (2 oz) mushrooms,
  sliced
salt and black pepper

SERVES 1

METHOD Heat the oil in an omelette pan on the hotplate. With a balloon whisk, whisk the eggs with 1 tablespoon water and salt and pepper until frothy. Pour the egg mixture into the pan. Move gently with a palette knife, pulling the mixture from the sides to the centre as it sets and letting the liquid in the centre run to the sides. When almost cooked sprinkle on the cheese and mushrooms.

Using the palette knife, loosen the omelette from the sides of the pan and gently fold in half before slipping it on to a warmed plate. Serve with a side salad.

Parsnips Country Style

This recipe uses a blue-veined Cheshire or Stilton cheese but any similar cheese would be suitable.

500 g (1 lb) young parsnips, boiled or braised	*Cheshire or Stilton cheese*	*freshly milled black pepper*
75 g (3 oz) blue-veined	*50 g (2 oz) walnuts, chopped*	

SERVES 4

METHOD Strain the parsnips and return to the warm saucepan they were cooked in. Add the cheese, walnuts and pepper. Toss gently – the heat of the saucepan will soften the cheese. Serve immediately.

Rice and Broccoli Stir-Fry

This is a crisp and healthy way to serve broccoli. White or brown rice may be used.

1.5 litres (2½ pints) water	*250 g (8 oz) broccoli florets*	*2 tablespoons dark soya sauce*
250 g (8 oz) brown or white basmati rice	*½ red pepper, sliced thinly*	*1 tablespoon sesame seeds*
3 tablespoons safflower oil	*1 tablespoon sesame oil*	*salt*

SERVES 4

METHOD Bring the water to the boil and add 1 teaspoon salt. Add the rice and cook for 8–10 minutes for white rice, 30–35 minutes for brown. Strain, rinse with hot water and spread out to dry on a baking sheet.

Heat the safflower oil in a wok or heavy-based saucepan and quickly fry the broccoli and red pepper, stirring all the time, for 5 minutes.

Add the rice, sesame oil, soya sauce and sesame seeds. Cook for a further 2 minutes and serve.

The Baker's Oven

This chapter contains four pastry recipes. Many people lack confidence when it comes to pastry-making, so a pâte brisée recipe which will never fail seemed a must! Choux pastry is a popular choice which can be used for a range of dishes, and hot water crust pastry follows a very similar technique. Finally, to make a shortcrust with a difference, there is a walnut pastry. Try these simple recipes and you will discover the delights of making pies, tarts and flans for the family.

Drop Scones

These scones can be cooked directly on the hotplate.

200 g (7 oz) plain wholemeal flour	50 g (2 oz) caster sugar	1 teaspoon grated orange zest
1 teaspoon baking powder	25 g (1 oz) butter	50 g (2 oz) raisins
½ teaspoon cinnamon	2 eggs	
	300 ml (½ pint) milk	

MAKES APPROXIMATELY 25

METHOD In a large bowl, mix together the flour, baking powder, cinnamon and caster sugar. Rub in the butter until the mixture resembles fine breadcrumbs.

Beat the eggs with the milk and add to the mixture with the orange zest.

Set the cooker on the hotplate mode and lightly oil the hotplate.

Drop small quantities (about 1 tablespoon) of the batter on to the hotplate. Sprinkle on the raisins.

Cook for 2–3 minutes until bubbles appear, then, using a palette knife, turn the scones over and cook the other side.

Serve hot or cold.

Pâte Brisée

This is my favourite lining pastry.

Container	20 cm (8-inch)	25 cm (10-inch)	30 cm (12-inch)
plain flour	125 g (4 oz)	190 g (6 ½ oz)	250 g (8 oz)
butter	50 g (2 oz)	100 g (3 ½ oz)	125 g (4 oz)
egg yolks	1	1	2
salt	pinch	pinch	½ teaspoon
water	1 ½–2	2 ½–3	3 ½–4
tablespoons	tablespoons	tablespoons	

METHOD   The butter should be at room temperature, so utilize the warmth of the hotplate if the butter is taken straight out of the refrigerator.

Place all the ingredients in a bowl with the smaller measurement of water. Using one hand only, mix the ingredients together with your fingers to form a moist paste. If the mixture is too dry, add the remaining ½ tablespoon of water.

Gently knead the pastry on a floured surface. The glutinous quality will quickly disappear but the pastry will remain pliable. Chill for 30 minutes before use. Use the same day.

Hot Water Crust Pastry

This makes enough pastry for Lamb Pies (page 52). Double the quantity for a traditional 10 × 25 cm (4 × 10 inch) raised pie, or to line an 18–20 cm (7–8 inch) springform tin.

125 g (4 oz) butter	*125 ml (4 fl oz) milk and water, mixed*	*250 g (8 oz) plain flour*

MAKES 250 g (8 OZ) PASTRY

METHOD   Put the milk and water and butter in a saucepan and melt the butter on the cool part of the hotplate. Move to the hottest part of the hotplate to bring the liquid to the boil.

Remove from the heat and immediately add the flour, mixing well.

Leave in the saucepan to keep warm – the pastry is easier to work with before it cools.

Raspberry Tart

pâte brisée pastry for a
  25 cm (10-inch) flan
  (page 65) or 175 g (6 oz)
  shortcrust pastry
2–3 tablespoons raspberry
  jam

125 g (4 oz) raspberries,
  fresh or frozen
caster sugar
For the frangipane:
100 g (3 ½ oz) butter
100 g (3 ½ oz) caster sugar
1 egg, beaten

1 egg yolk
100 g (3 ½ oz) ground
  almonds
25 g (1 oz) plain flour
2 tablespoons framboise
  (raspberry liqueur)

SERVES 8–10   **OVEN TEMPERATURE 180°C**

METHOD Preheat the main oven to 180°C. To prepare the frangipane, cream the butter and sugar together until light and creamy. Beat the whole egg and egg yolk together and add to the mixture a little at a time. Stir in the ground almonds, flour and framboise.

To prepare the raspberry tart, roll out the pastry on a floured surface and line a greased 25 cm (10-inch) flan tin. Spread the raspberry jam thinly over the base of the pastry. Cover evenly with the frangipane. Scatter the raspberries over the surface and bake for 40–45 minutes. Ten minutes before the end of the cooking time, sprinkle the surface of the tart with caster sugar.

Apple and Raisin Cake

This delicious cake becomes more sticky if kept in an airtight tin for two days.

125 g (4 oz) butter
175 g (6 oz) soft brown
  sugar
1 egg, beaten
½ teaspoon vanilla essence

3 cooking apples, peeled,
  cored, sliced and cooked to
  a thick purée
250 g (8 oz) self-raising
  flour, sifted

1 teaspoon bicarbonate of
  soda
2 teaspoons mixed spice
½ teaspoon salt
175 g (6 oz) raisins

MAKES AN 18 CM (7-INCH) ROUND CAKE   **OVEN TEMPERATURE 160°C**

METHOD Preheat the main oven to 160°C. Grease and line an 18 cm (7-inch) round deep cake tin with greased greaseproof paper.

Beat the butter and sugar together and add the egg and vanilla essence. Stir in the apple and fold in the flour, bicarbonate of soda, mixed spice and salt. Add the raisins. Bake in the centre of the oven for 50–60 minutes, until the cake is nicely brown and is leaving the sides of the tin.

Choux Pastry

The 2-egg quantity will make approximately 12 eclairs or 20–25 profiteroles; the 3-egg quantity will make approximately 18 eclairs or 30–35 profiteroles.

	2-egg mixture	*3-egg mixture*
water	*150 ml (5 fl oz)*	*225 ml (7½ fl oz)*
butter	*50 g (2 oz)*	*75 g (3 oz)*
plain flour, sifted	*65 g (2½ oz)*	*100 g (3½ oz)*
salt	*pinch*	*pinch*
eggs	*2*	*3*

METHOD Put the water and butter in a saucepan and melt the butter on the cool part of the hotplate. Move the saucepan to the hottest part of the hotplate and bring the liquid to the boil.

Immediately add the sifted flour and salt, all in one go, and mix well. Remove the saucepan from the heat. The mixture will form a smooth paste in the shape of a ball.

Beat the eggs and add a little at a time, beating well after each addition. Use immediately.

Crunchy Ham and Corn Flan

175 g (6 oz) shortcrust pastry, white or wholemeal (page 69)	*300 ml (½ pint) milk*	*50 g (2 oz) fresh breadcrumbs*
20 g (¾ oz) butter	*75 g (3 oz) cooked ham, off the bone*	*50 g (2 oz) Cheddar cheese, grated*
20 g (¾ oz) plain flour	*175 g (6 oz) sweetcorn*	*salt and black pepper*
	1 tablespoon chopped parsley	

SERVES 4–6   **OVEN TEMPERATURE 200°C**

METHOD Preheat the main oven to 200°C. Roll out the pastry on a floured surface and line a greased 20 cm (8-inch) flan dish or ring. Prick the base lightly.

Make a sauce by melting the butter in a saucepan. Stir in the flour and cook for 2–3 minutes. Remove the saucepan from the heat and slowly mix in the milk, stirring continuously. Season with salt and pepper and return the pan to the heat to thicken the sauce.

Stir in the chopped ham and sweetcorn, then pour into the pastry shell. Mix together the pastry, breadcrumbs and grated cheese and sprinkle over the filling.

Bake until golden brown, 35–40 minutes. Serve hot.

Neil's Potato Cakes

A recipe to use up left-over potatoes – ideal for freezing uncooked.

175 g (6 oz) self-raising flour	*50 g (2 oz) butter*	*1 egg, beaten*
pinch of salt	*300 g (10 oz) potatoes, cooked*	

MAKES 10 **OVEN TEMPERATURE 190°C**

METHOD Preheat the main oven to 190°C. Place the flour and salt in a bowl and rub in the butter. Mix in the potatoes. Add the beaten egg and mix to a soft, pliable dough.

On a floured surface, roll out the dough to 1 cm (½ inch) thick. Cut into rounds of 5–8 cm (2–3 inches). Place on a greased baking sheet and bake for 30 minutes.

Serve the potato cakes while they are warm.

Walnut Pastry

A mixture of hard margarine and vegetable fat makes a pastry that is easy to handle; a mixture of butter and vegetable fat will have a better flavour, but is a little more difficult to handle. The amount of water required will vary enormously as different flours absorb different amounts – a wholemeal flour pastry will require more water than one made with white flour. To line an 18–20 cm (7–8 inch) flan tin, use 125 g (4 oz) pastry; for a 25–30 cm (10–12 inch) flan tin, use 250 g (8 oz) pastry.

	for 125 g (4 oz) pastry	*for 250 g (8 oz) pastry*
white plain flour	*50 g (2 oz)*	*125 g (4 oz)*
wholemeal plain flour	*50 g (2 oz)*	*125 g (4 oz)*
salt	*pinch*	*pinch*
hard margarine or butter	*25 g (1 oz)*	*50 g (2 oz)*
vegetable fat	*25 g (1 oz)*	*50 g (2 oz)*
walnuts, chopped very finely	*25 g (1 oz)*	*50 g (2 oz)*
water	*1½–2 tablespoons*	*3–3½ tablespoons*

METHOD Sift the flour and salt into a bowl. Add the fats and, using a round-ended knife, chop finely.

Rub the fat into the flour with the fingertips. When the mixture resembles fine breadcrumbs stir in the nuts.

Add the water and mix, first using the knife, then the fingertips. Wrap in cling film and store in the refrigerator for at least 30 minutes before using.

SHORTCRUST PASTRY Use either wholemeal plain or white plain flour and ingredients as above, omitting the walnuts.

Flowerpot Loaves

This recipe always creates great amusement, for the bread is baked in 10-13 cm (4-5-inch) clay flowerpots (although if you prefer you can make it in loaf tins). It is a 'one rise' dough so it will suit a busy household. If the flowerpots are new grease them inside and out and bake empty in a hot oven prior to use. I use fresh or easy-blend yeast depending on availability.

250 g (8 oz) strong plain white flour	*250 g (8 oz) strong plain wholemeal flour*	*25 g (1 oz) fresh yeast or 1 sachet of easy-blend yeast*
1 teaspoon salt	*1 teaspoon caster sugar*	*cracked wheat or crushed cornflakes, to decorate*
	15 g (½ oz) butter (optional)	
	300 ml (½ pint) water	

MAKES 2 × 500 g (1 LB) LOAVES   **OVEN TEMPERATURE 230°C**

METHOD Preheat the main oven to 230°C. Sift the white flour and salt into a bowl. Stir in the wholemeal flour, sugar and easy-blend yeast, if using. Rub the butter in with your fingertips, if using (this makes a softer dough).

Use the warmth of the hotplate to take the chill off the water – it is not necessary to use hand-hot liquids for this type of recipe.

If using fresh yeast, crumble into the water at this stage.

Add the liquid to the flour and mix to a soft dough. Knead on a floured surface for 5 minutes only. Divide into 2 equal portions, shape and place in the greased flowerpots. Brush the tops lightly with salted water and sprinkle on the cracked wheat or cornflakes.

Place the flowerpots in a lightly oiled polythene bag, tie loosely and leave to rise until the dough is double in size. A yeast dough does not require warmth to work – it will rise in the refrigerator, but will take longer.

Bake for 30–35 minutes. Test by tapping the loaves – if they sound hollow they are baked.

NOTE If using 2 × 500 g (1 lb) loaf tins, divide the mixture into 2 equal halves then each half into 4 pieces. Roll each piece into a smooth, round ball. Place four balls into each greased tin, close together in a row, to produce 4 small 'Hovis' shapes.

Waterford Special Brown Soda Bread

Waterford in Ireland is the home of the Stanley Cooker and this recipe for Brown Soda Bread was given to me while I was visiting the foundry. Soda bread could almost be called instant bread, it is so quick to make. Like all home-made breads, it must be eaten when fresh. If buttermilk is not available, use fresh milk and add 1 teaspoon cream of tartar.

125 g (4 oz) strong plain white flour	*1 teaspoon bicarbonate of soda*	*1 egg (optional)*
1 teaspoon salt	*375 g (12 oz) strong plain wholemeal flour*	*300 ml (½ pint) buttermilk*

MAKES AN 800 g (1 LB 10 OZ) LOAF	**OVEN TEMPERATURE 200°C**

METHOD Preheat the main oven to 200°C. Sift the white flour, salt and bicarbonate of soda into a bowl and stir in the wholemeal flour.

If using egg, mix the egg and buttermilk together and add to the flours to make a soft dough.

On a floured surface, lightly knead until smooth. Shape into a 18 cm (7-inch) round and place on a greased and floured baking sheet.

Mark the top with a cross, using either a sharp knife or the floured handle of a wooden spoon.

Bake for 40–45 minutes.

Picnic Tart

This makes a lovely supper dish and is very good for 'carrying out' – a firm favourite in school sandwich boxes.

125 g (4 oz) walnut pastry (page 69) or shortcrust pastry	*1 onion, chopped*	*125 g (4 oz) Cheddar cheese, grated*
1 tablespoon oil for frying	*2 courgettes, sliced*	*½ teaspoon dried mustard powder*
25 g (1 oz) butter	*2 eggs*	*salt and pepper*
	2 tomatoes, skinned, de-seeded and chopped	

SERVES 4–6	**OVEN TEMPERATURE 200°C**

METHOD Preheat the oven to 200°C. Roll out the pastry on a floured surface and use to line a greased 18 cm (7-inch) flan ring, placed on a greased baking sheet.

If using the walnut pastry, press the base down firmly, using your fingertips. Check that there are no gaps between the nuts and pastry for the filling to seep through. You may bake the pastry shell blind for 10 minutes before using to firm the pastry base, but there should be no need if the nuts are finely chopped.

Heat the oil and butter in a frying-pan and gently cook the onion and courgettes until soft. Beat the eggs in a bowl and add the onion, courgettes, tomatoes, cheese and mustard and season with salt and pepper. Pour into the flan case and bake for 35–40 minutes. Serve hot or cold.

Victoria Sandwich

This basic recipe for a Victoria sandwich could be adapted by adding your own favourite flavourings.

For an 18 cm (7-inch) Victoria sandwich:
125 g (4 oz) butter or soft margarine
125 g (4 oz) caster sugar
2 eggs (size 2), beaten lightly

125 g (4 oz) self-raising flour, sifted
For a 20 cm (8-inch) Victoria sandwich:
175 g (6 oz) butter or soft margarine
175 g (6 oz) caster sugar

3 eggs (size 2), beaten lightly
175 g (6 oz) self-raising flour, sifted
To finish:
4 tablespoons raspberry jam
caster sugar for dusting

MAKES AN 18 CM (7-INCH) OR A 20 CM (8-INCH) CAKE   OVEN TEMPERATURE 180°C

METHOD Preheat the main oven to 180°C. Lightly grease two sandwich tins of the appropriate measurement and line with greased greaseproof paper or non-stick baking parchment.

Cream the butter or soft margarine with the sugar until light and fluffy. Add the beaten eggs gradually. Fold in the flour. Spread the mixture between the two sandwich tins. Bake in the centre of the oven for 20–25 minutes, until the cakes spring back when lightly pressed.

Turn the cakes out of the tins and cool on a wire rack. When cool, spread one cake with the raspberry jam and place the other cake on top. Finish by dusting with a little caster sugar.

Christmas Cake

There are many variations in the ingredients of a rich fruit cake, but this is a good basic recipe. It is best made about eight weeks before Christmas.

175 g (6 oz) butter or soft margarine
175 g (6 oz) soft brown sugar
4 eggs (size 2), beaten
175 g (6 oz) plain flour, sifted
½ teaspoon mixed spice

grated zest of ½ orange
grated zest and juice of 1 lemon
250 g (8 oz) currants
250 g (8 oz) sultanas
250 g (8 oz) raisins
125 g (4 oz) glacé cherries, halved

50 g (2 oz) mixed peel, chopped finely
25 g (1 oz) almonds, chopped
25 g (1 oz) ground almonds
1 dessertspoon treacle

MAKES A 20 CM (8-INCH) ROUND CAKE OR AN 18 CM (7-INCH) SQUARE CAKE

OVEN TEMPERATURE 140°C

METHOD Preheat the main oven to 140°C. Grease a 20 cm (8-inch) round cake tin or an 18 cm (7-inch) square tin and line with greased greaseproof paper.

Cream the butter or margarine with the sugar until light and fluffy. Gradually beat in the eggs, adding a tablespoon of flour after each addition if the mixture starts to curdle a little.

Fold in the flour and mixed spice, followed by the fruit and nuts and finally the treacle.

Spoon the mixture into the prepared cake tin and spread out evenly. Bake in the main oven for about 4 hours. When the cake is cooked a skewer inserted into the centre should come out clean. Return to the oven for a further 30 minutes if required.

Leave in the tin to cool before removing and wrapping well in double greaseproof paper. Store in an airtight tin. 'Feed' with brandy in the weeks leading up to Christmas.

Coconut Chocolate Bake

A very popular tray bake which children love.

For the base:
150 g (5 oz) butter
125 g (4 oz) caster sugar
1 tablespoon syrup
2 teaspoons cocoa powder

50 g (2 oz) desiccated
coconut
1½ teaspoons baking powder,
175 g (6 oz) plain flour

For the icing:
125 g (4 oz) icing sugar,
sifted
15 g (½ oz) butter
1 teaspoon cocoa powder
1 teaspoon vanilla essence
2–3 teaspoons hot water

MAKES 16 FINGERS	OVEN TEMPERATURE 190°C

METHOD Preheat the main oven to 190°C. Grease a 29 × 19 cm (11½ × 7½-inch) swiss roll tin. Put the butter, sugar, syrup and cocoa powder into a medium-size saucepan and place on the hotplate to melt. When melted add the coconut. Sift together the flour and baking powder, add to the pan and mix well. Pour the mixture into the swiss roll tin and spread out evenly. Bake in the centre of the oven for about 10 minutes.

Remove the base from the oven. Beat all the icing ingredients together until smooth and pour over the base while it is still hot. Cut into fingers while the tray bake is still warm. When cold, remove from the tin.

Sultana Scones

There are many recipes for scones – this one is a particular favourite in my family.

125 g (4 oz) self-raising
flour
125 g (4 oz) self-raising
wholemeal flour

½ teaspoon cream of tartar
¼ teaspoon bicarbonate of
soda
25 g (1 oz) butter
50 g (2 oz) caster sugar

50 g (2 oz) sultanas
1 egg, beaten
approx 150 ml (¼ pint)
milk

MAKES 10	OVEN TEMPERATURE 220°C

METHOD Preheat the main oven to 220°C. Lightly grease a baking sheet.

Sift together the flour, cream of tartar and bicarbonate of soda. Rub the fat into the flour until the mixture resembles breadcrumbs. Add the sugar and the sultanas. Mix the egg and milk together and add sufficient to make a soft dough. Turn on to a lightly floured surface and knead gently. Roll out to 2 cm (¾ inch) thick. Cut into rounds with a 5 cm (2-inch) fluted cutter. Arrange on the greased baking sheet. Brush the tops with a little milk.

Bake towards the top of the oven for 10–15 minutes. Split and butter when cool.

Puddings & Desserts

Planning a meal is rather like choosing an outfit to wear – what will complement and what will clash? Your pudding or dessert should put the finishing touches to the meal, providing a final balance of flavour, colour and texture. Your final course can be a simple affair or the result of hours of work that will be eaten in seconds! Whatever you choose your versatile two-oven Stanley will meet your demands with ease, leaving you free to enjoy sharing the meal with friends or family.

Redcurrant Tart

There are two ways of presenting this recipe, both of which achieve a spectacular effect.

pâte brisée for a 30 cm (12-inch) flan (page 65)	*500 g (1 lb) redcurrants* *175 g (6 oz) caster sugar*	*a little redcurrant jam* *2 egg whites*

SERVES 8–10   **OVEN TEMPERATURE 190°C/220°C**

METHOD Preheat the main oven to 190°C. Roll out the pastry on a floured surface and line a greased 30 cm (12-inch) flan tin. Prick the bastry base all over with a fork. Line the uncooked pastry shell with greaseproof paper and sprinkle in some dried beans or rice. Bake blind for 20 minutes, removing the beans or rice and greaseproof paper after 15 minutes. Remove from the oven and raise the temperature to 220°C.

On the hotplate, gently simmer the redcurrants with 50 g (2 oz) sugar in 1 tablespoon water for 2 minutes. Strain and allow to cool.

Brush the pastry base with a little redcurrant jam. Arrange the redcurrants in a single layer on top.

Whisk the egg whites until they hold their shape. Whisk in 50 g (2 oz) sugar until the egg whites are smooth and glossy. With the 'cutting' edge of a metal spoon, gently cut and fold in the remaining 50 g (2 oz) sugar.

Fit a large piping bag with a star nozzle and fill with meringue. Pipe the meringue in criss-cross lines (lattice effect) over the redcurrants.

Bake the tart until the meringue is slightly coloured, 5–10 minutes. Serve hot or cold.

ALTERNATIVE PRESENTATION: Roll the pastry out to fit the base of a swiss roll tin and present the tart as a rectangular shape.

Apricot Whirligig

A tasty way to dress up stewed apple which is very popular with children.

1 large cooking apple, peeled, cored and sliced	125 g (4 oz) plain flour	1 teaspoon cream of tartar
4 tablespoons apricot jam	½ teaspoon bicarbonate of soda	25 g (1 oz) butter
		4–6 tablespoons milk

SERVES 4 **OVEN TEMPERATURE 220°C**

METHOD Preheat the main oven to 220°C. Place the apple slices in a straight-sided glass ovenproof dish, size approximately 900 ml (1½ pints). Spread 1 tablespoon apricot jam over the surface of the apples and bake for 10 minutes.

Sift the flour into a bowl with the bicarbonate of soda and cream of tartar. Rub the butter in with the fingertips. Add the milk and mix to a soft dough.

On a floured surface, roll out the dough to a rectangle 20 × 15 cm (8 × 6 inches). Spread thinly with apricot jam.

Roll up swiss roll fashion and cut into 8 slices. Place the slices on top of the partially baked apples, laying them flat with a space in between each slice to allow them to rise a little.

Return to the oven and bake for 15 minutes. Serve with home-made custard or cream.

Spicy Apple Charlotte

Layering the fruit and crumbs gives extra attraction to a charlotte. I use an ovenproof glass serving dish so that everyone can see the layers. Try a combination of damsons and cinnamon as an alternative.

500 g (1 lb) cooking apples, peeled, cored and sliced	125 g (4 oz) caster sugar	1 teaspoon ground ginger
grated zest and juice of 1 lemon	125 g (4 oz) fresh breadcrumbs	50 g (2 oz) butter, melted

SERVES 4 **OVEN TEMPERATURE 180°C**

METHOD Preheat the main oven to 180°C. Place the apple slices in a bowl with the lemon juice, stirring carefully to make sure they are completely coated. In another bowl, mix together the lemon zest, sugar, breadcrumbs and ginger.

Place alternate layers of apples and breadcrumbs in the ovenproof dish, finishing with a breadcrumb layer. Pour the melted butter over the surface and bake for 30–40 minutes. The top should crisp nicely.

Serve with whipped cream with a little stem ginger folded into it. As a healthy alternative, use fat-free fromage frais.

Crème Caramel

This is a classic dish which is popular with all age groups. It can be made the day before you are entertaining and stored in a refrigerator. I often make it at the same time as a pavlova, using up the three egg yolks left over from the meringue. You can use just one or two extra yolks if you like.

For the caramel:	*For the custard:*	*40 g (1½ oz) caster sugar*
5 tablespoons water	*4 eggs (size 2)*	*½ teaspoon vanilla essence*
150 g (5 oz) caster sugar	*3 egg yolks (size 2)*	*600 ml (1 pint) milk*

SERVES 4–6   **OVEN TEMPERATURE 160°C**

METHOD Preheat the main oven to 160°C. To make the caramel, put the sugar and water in a heavy-based saucepan and place on the simmering plate to dissolve. When the sugar has dissolved, transfer to the hotplate and bring to the boil without stirring. Boil steadily until the syrup turns a golden brown colour. Pour at once into a lightly oiled 1.2-litre (2-pint) ovenproof dish or mould and allow to set.

To make the custard, lightly whisk the eggs, sugar and vanilla essence together. Heat the milk in a saucepan on the hotplate until tepid. Pour on to the egg mixture and mix well. Strain the custard into the dish and allow any bubbles to subside.

Cover the dish with a piece of aluminium foil and place in a bain-marie. Cook in the main oven for about 1–1½ hours.

Allow the custard to go cold, preferably overnight in a refrigerator, before gently releasing from the dish or mould.

Strawberry Choux Gâteau

This versatile pastry makes a delightful summer dessert.

3-egg quantity of choux pastry (page 68)	*150 ml (¼ pint) double cream, whipped*	***To decorate:***
50 g (2 oz) plain cooking chocolate, chopped into 5–8 mm (⅛–¼-inch) pieces	*150 ml (¼ pint) strawberry yogurt*	*plain cooking chocolate*
	175 g (6 oz) strawberries, sliced	*a few whole strawberries*
		a little whipped cream
		icing sugar for dusting

SERVES 6–8   **OVEN TEMPERATURE 220°C**

METHOD Preheat the main oven to 220°C. Divide the pastry in half and spread on to a greased and floured baking sheet in 2 × 18 cm (7-inch) circles. Smooth the top lightly and sprinkle on the chopped chocolate. Bake for 10 minutes, then reduce the heat to 190°C

and bake for a further 20–25 minutes. Leave to cool.

Whip the cream and fold in the yogurt and strawberries. Sandwich the two rounds of pastry together with the cream filling.

TO DECORATE, melt a little chocolate on the simmering hotplate. Dip the strawberries into the chocolate, coating two-thirds of the fruit. Leave to set. Dust the top of the gâteau with icing sugar and pipe rosettes of whipped cream around the edge. Place a chocolate-coated strawberry on top of each rosette.

Fruity Bread and Butter Pudding

An old favourite is given a modern, healthy emphasis.

50 g (2 oz) low-fat spread or butter	*75 g (3 oz) no-soak dried apricots, chopped*	*50 g (2 oz) light brown sugar*
4 thin slices of wholemeal bread	*25 g (1 oz) sultanas*	*450 ml (¾ pint) milk*
	2 eggs	*25 g (1 oz) demerara sugar*

SERVES 4   **OVEN TEMPERATURE 160°C**

METHOD Preheat the main oven to 160°C. Spread the low-fat spread or butter on to the bread and cut into triangles. Grease a 900 ml (1½-pint) oval ovenproof dish and arrange a layer of bread on the base. Sprinkle on half the apricots and sultanas. Repeat the layers with the fruit and bread, finishing with a layer of bread.

Beat the eggs and light brown sugar together. Bring the milk to the boil and whisk into the eggs thoroughly. Strain the custard mixture over the bread and leave to stand for 20–30 minutes. Sprinkle the demerara sugar on the top and bake uncovered in a bain-marie for 1–1¼ hours.

Damson Brûlée

A very popular dessert in our family. The intense flavour of the damsons topped with the whipped cream and the brûlée is delicious. The brûlée can easily be made on the hotplate and the whole dish can be prepared the day before it is required.

500 g (1 lb) damsons, cooked and cooled	*cream, whipped*	*sugar*
	For the brûlée:	*4 tablespoons water*
300 ml (½ pint) double	*125 g (4 oz) granulated*	

SERVES 6

METHOD Place the damsons in a 1.2-litre (2-pint) soufflé dish. Spread the whipped cream over the top. Place in a freezer for at least 3 hours until the cream is hard.

To make the brûlée, place the sugar and water in a heavy-based saucepan on the simmering plate. Allow the sugar to dissolve, then transfer to the hotplate and bring to the boil. Boil steadily until the syrup turns a pale golden brown colour.

Remove from the hotplate and allow to cool for a few moments. Remove the damsons from the freezer and pour the brûlée over the top. Refrigerate for 3 hours or overnight before serving.

Compote of Autumn Fruits

A selection of autumn fruits cooked in a syrup of apple juice and honey.

500 g (1 lb) Victoria plums, halved and stoned

500 g (1 lb) pears, peeled, halved and cored
125 g (4 oz) blackberries

150 ml (¼ pint) unsweetened apple juice
2 tablespoons clear honey
a pinch of cinnamon

SERVES 6

METHOD Layer the plums and pears in an ovenproof dish. Sprinkle the blackberries over the top.

In a small saucepan, heat the apple juice and honey together with the cinnamon. Pour over the fruit.

Cook gently in the lower oven for 1–2 hours, dependent on the level of heat.

Raspberry Soufflé

A very simple and light dessert which is ideal after a rich main course. Any soft fruit can be used, strawberries, cooked blackcurrants or redcurrants or a mixture.

2 egg whites
125 g (4 oz) caster sugar

375 g (12 oz) raspberries, mashed

SERVES 4   **OVEN TEMPERATURE 190°C**

METHOD Preheat the main oven to 190°C. Whisk the egg whites until they reach the stiff peak stage. Add the caster sugar 1 tablespoon at a time, whisking after each addition. Fold in the mashed fruit and pour into a greased 900 ml (1½–pint) soufflé or ovenproof dish.

Place in the centre of the oven for about 12 minutes, until the soufflé has risen and is lightly brown on the top.

Kiwi and Raspberry Trifle

During the Christmas period I replace the raspberries with satsumas.

1 raspberry-jam-flavoured
 swiss roll
4 tablespoons vermouth
4 kiwi fruit, peeled and
 sliced
125 g (4 oz) raspberries

75 g (3 oz) ratafia biscuits
300 ml (½ pint) whipping
 cream
For the crème patissière:
1 egg
1 egg yolk

50 g (2 oz) caster sugar
25 g (1 oz) plain flour
300 ml (½ pint) milk

SERVES 4 –6

METHOD Cut the swiss roll into slices and cover the base of a suitable serving dish. Moisten with the vermouth.

Layer the fruits and ratafia biscuits over the swiss roll, reserving several biscuits, raspberries and slices of kiwi fruit to use as decoration.

To make the crème patissière, beat the whole egg and the egg yolk together. Add the sugar and flour and cream well together.

Heat the milk slightly and blend it in to the creamed mixture. Return to the pan and stir until boiling. (The flour prevents curdling.) Pour over the fruit and biscuits. Chill.

Decorate with whipped cream and the reserved fruit and biscuit.

Spiced Apple Meringue

500 g (1 lb) cooking apples,
 peeled, cored and sliced
zest and juice of 1 orange
150 g (5 oz) caster sugar

50 g (2 oz) raisins
50 g (2 oz) butter
125 g (4 oz) cake crumbs
50 g (2 oz) soft brown sugar

½ teaspoon cinnamon
2 tablespoons orange
 marmalade
2 egg whites

SERVES 4 **OVEN TEMPERATURE 160°C**

METHOD Preheat the main oven to 160°C. Place the apples and orange zest and juice in a saucepan with 25 g (1 oz) caster sugar. Cover and simmer gently for 10 minutes, or until the apples are cooked. Stir in the raisins. Melt the butter in a frying-pan. Mix together the cake crumbs, soft brown sugar and cinnamon. Add to the frying-pan and cook gently, stirring, to absorb the butter, until the mixture browns lightly. Place the crumb mixture on the base of an ovenproof dish. Carefully spread the marmalade and then the apples on top of the crumb mixture. Whisk the egg whites until soft and dry. Whisk in 50 g (2 oz) sugar, then fold in the remaining sugar. Spoon on top of the apples and bake for 30 minutes.

If the main oven is in use this recipe could be cooked in the lower oven, depending on the main oven setting.

Summer Menu

Chilled Tomato and Celery Soup

♦

Oven-Baked Salmon served with new potatoes and mange tout

♦

Asparagus with Hollandaise Sauce

♦

Lemon Pavlova

Chilled Tomato and Celery Soup

1 head of celery, cleaned and
    chopped
1 onion, chopped
450 ml (¾ pint) vegetable
    stock (page 19)

1 tablespoon tomato purée
750 g (1½ lb) tomatoes,
    skinned, de-seeded and
    chopped
juice of 1 lemon

To garnish:
celery leaves
strands of lemon zest

SERVES 4

METHOD Put the celery, onion and stock in a saucepan and bring to the boil. Move to the simmering plate and simmer, covered, for 30 minutes, or until the vegetables are soft. Purée in a blender or food processor.

Return to the pan and add the tomato purée, tomatoes and lemon juice. Simmer for 10 minutes. Chill thoroughly.

Serve garnished with a small celery leaf and strands of lemon zest, cut using a canelle knife or lemon zester.

Oven-Baked Salmon

50 g (2 oz) butter	*750 g (1 ½ lb) middle-cut salmon*	*1 lemon, sliced* *freshly milled black pepper*

SERVES 4 **OVEN TEMPERATURE 150°C**

METHOD Preheat the main oven to 150°C. Use half the butter to grease a double sheet of aluminium foil. Place the fish in the centre and smear the remaining butter over the surface. Sprinkle the cavity with freshly milled black pepper and fill with lemon slices. Wrap the fish loosely in the aluminium foil and seal tightly. Place in a shallow roasting tin and bake for 30 minutes.

Remove the skin while it is still warm, but allow the fish to rest for 10 minutes before serving.

NOTE If you intend to serve this fish cold, replace the butter with 2 tablespoons light oil.

Hollandaise Sauce

This sauce is to serve with the oven-baked salmon, or indeed any fish dish. If you are going to use it to accompany any other type of food, replace the fish stock with lemon juice. Orange-flavoured Hollandaise sauce goes well with asparagus.

3 egg yolks *2 tablespoons fish stock (see page 20)*	*1 tablespoon white wine vinegar* *175 g (6 oz) unsalted butter*	*salt and pepper*

MAKES 300 ML (½ PINT)

METHOD In a glass bowl, whisk together the egg yolks, fish stock and white wine vinegar with 1 tablespoon water. Put the bowl to fit snugly on a saucepan of simmering water on the hotplate. The base of the bowl must not touch the water. Whisk until the sauce thickens and the whisk leaves a trail. It should take no more than 5 minutes.

Remove from the heat and whisk in the butter, piece by piece. Season with salt and pepper, remembering that the fish stock has already been seasoned.

This sauce can be kept warm for 20 minutes; cover and place on the hob or in the lower oven away from extreme heat. Stir occasionally.

Pictured over page: Chilled Tomato and Celery Soup
Oven-Baked Salmon, served with new potatoes and mange tout
Asparagus with Hollandaise Sauce
Lemon Pavlova

Lemon Pavlova

A delicious crispy meringue with a marshmallow centre. The egg yolks are used to make the lemon topping.

3 egg whites
175 g (6 oz) caster sugar
1 small teaspoon vanilla
* essence*
1 small teaspon white
* vinegar*

For the lemon topping:
3 egg yolks
75 g (3 oz) caster sugar
grated zest and juice of 1
* lemon*

300 ml (½ pint) whipping
* cream*
To decorate:
1 lemon, sliced
grated lemon zest

SERVES 6   **OVEN TEMPERATURE 150°C**

METHOD Preheat the main oven to 150°C. Cover a baking sheet with a piece of aluminium foil and oil lightly.

Place the egg whites in a large bowl and whisk until the stiff peak stage. Whisk in 1 tablespoon of sugar at a time until you have a stiff meringue. Add the vanilla essence and the white vinegar.

Turn the meringue out on to the baking sheet and make a 15–18 cm (6–7-inch) round. Bake for 30 minutes then turn the oven off and leave the meringue in it for 1½–2 hours. (You may be able to use the lower oven, depending on the mode your cooker is operating on.)

When cold, carefully remove from the baking sheet and place in a suitable serving dish.

To prepare the lemon topping, beat the egg yolks and sugar together in a glass bowl until light. Mix in the lemon zest and juice. Fit the bowl snugly on to a saucepan of simmering water on the hotplate. Cook gently until the mixture thickens, stirring all the time.

Allow to cool, then fold into the whipped cream. Spoon on to the pavlova and decorate with twisted lemon slices and grated lemon zest.

Winter Menu

Parsnip and Pear soup
Lemon Roast Turkey
Fan-Shaped Roast Potatoes
Honey–Baked Carrots
Granny's Christmas pudding
Dundee Mince Tart

Parsnip and Pear Soup

An unusual combination which makes a deliciously warming soup for a cold day.

25 g (1 oz) butter	*2 large Conference pears,*	*salt and pepper*
375 g (12 oz) parsnips,	*peeled, cored and chopped*	*chopped parsley, to garnish*
chopped	*600 ml (1 pint) light stock*	
1 onion, chopped	*300 ml (½ pint) milk*	

SERVES 6

METHOD Melt the butter in a large saucepan on the hotplate. Add the parsnips, onion and pears and fry gently until the onion is transparent. Add the stock and milk and bring slowly to the boil. Season with salt and pepper, cover and simmer gently on the coolest part of the hotplate for approximately 20–30 minutes, until the vegetables are tender.

Purée the soup in a blender or a food processor and check the seasoning. Garnish with the chopped parsley and serve with oven-baked croûtons.

Pictured over page
Parsnip and Pear Soup
Lemon Roast Turkey
Roast Fan Potatoes, Baked Honey Carrots
Granny's Christmas Pudding, Dundee Mince Tart

Lemon Roast Turkey

As a rough guide when choosing a turkey, remember that you need about 375 g (12 oz) per person, but turkey is always popular cold for sandwiches, etc. at Christmas.

175 g (6 oz) butter
zest and juice of 1 lemon

4 tablespoons chopped
parsley
6 kg (14 lb) turkey
1 onion, chopped finely

175 g (6 oz) breadcrumbs
1 egg
salt and pepper

SERVES 6, WITH PLENTY LEFT OVER FOR SANDWICHES   OVEN TEMPERATURE 160°C

METHOD   Preheat the oven to 160°C. To make the stuffing, cream together 125 g (4 oz) butter, half the lemon zest and juice and 1 tablespoon chopped parsley. Spoon under the skin at the neck end of the turkey, spreading evenly with your fingertips.

Fry the onion in the remaining butter until soft. Remove from the heat and mix thoroughly with the remaining parsley, lemon zest and juice, the breadcrumbs and the egg. Season with salt and pepper. Spoon the stuffing into the neck end of the turkey (do not overpack it). Fold the neck flap over. Truss loosely.

Place the turkey on a rack in a roasting tin to allow the juices to drain into the bottom of the tin for easy basting. Baste at regular intervals during cooking (see chart on page 00 for cooking times). To test if the turkey is cooked, pierce the thickest part of the leg with a thin skewer; the turkey is done if the juices run clear with no trace of pinkness.

Fan-Shaped Roast Potatoes

This is an attractive way to serve roast potatoes when entertaining.

1 kg (2 lb) potatoes, peeled
and cut into equal sizes

oil for roasting

SERVES 4   **OVEN TEMPERATURE 200°C**

METHOD   Preheat the main oven to 200°C. Starting at one end of the potato, using a sharp knife, cut halfway through at 3 mm (⅛ inch) intervals. Brush with oil and roast for 1 hour. The potato will open slightly during cooking.

Honey-Baked Carrots

750 g (1½ lb) carrots, peeled
  and cut into julienne
  strips
75 g (3 oz) butter, melted

3 tablespoons clear honey
3 tablespoons orange juice
1 tablespoon grated orange
  zest

salt and pepper
chopped parsley, to garnish

SERVES 6　　　　　　　　　　　　　　　　　**OVEN TEMPERATURE 190°C**

METHOD Preheat the main oven to 190°C. Place the carrots in a shallow ovenproof dish. Mix together the melted butter, honey and orange juice and zest. Pour over the carrots. Season with salt and pepper and cover with aluminium foil. Bake for 50–60 minutes or until tender.

NOTE New carrots can be left whole.

Granny's Christmas Pudding

A lovely light Christmas pudding which is best made about 6 - 8 weeks before Christmas. I like Christmas pudding too much to eat it only at Christmas, so we always have an extra one to enjoy on a cold January day. Alternatively, an attractively gift-wrapped home-made pudding makes a very acceptable present.

125 g (4 oz) fresh
  breadcrumbs
125 g (4 oz) self-raising
  flour, sifted
125 g (4 oz) suet
50 g (2 oz) cooking apples,
  peeled, cored and chopped
125 g (4 oz) currants

125 g (4 oz) sultanas
125 g (4 oz) raisins
25 g (1 oz) glacé cherries,
  quartered
125 g (4 oz) soft brown
  sugar
½ teaspoon mixed spice
25 g (1 oz) flaked almonds

1 tablespoon black treacle
juice of ½ lemon
juice of ½ orange
1 egg, lightly beaten
1 tablespoon brandy or dry
  sherry
200 ml (7 fl oz) Guinness

MAKES AN 1.5-LITRE (2½-PINT) PUDDING OR TWO SMALLER PUDDINGS

METHOD Mix all the dry ingredients together in a large bowl. Beat together the treacle, orange and lemon juice, eggs and brandy or sherry. Add to the dry ingredients with the Guinness and mix to a soft consistency. Cover the mixture and leave overnight.

The next day, grease 1 × 1.5-litre (2½-pint) pudding basin or 2 smaller basins. Stir the pudding mixture well and place in the basin(s). Cover with greased greaseproof paper and an aluminium foil lid. Place in a steamer, or lift into a large saucepan and pour some water half-way up the side of the basin(s). Place on the hotplate and cover with a lid. Bring to the boil and then remove to the coolest part of the hotplate for 6 hours. Top up the water with boiling water when necessary to maintain the temperature and also to prevent the pudding from drying up.

Alternatively, allow the pudding to come to the boil and then simmer for 30 minutes on the coolest part of the hotplate. Transfer the pan with the water to the lower oven for about 12 hours or overnight.

Dundee Mince Tart

This replaces the mince pie in my household. It can be cut into very small fingers for entertaining, 5 cm (2-inch) squares for family mince pies or 8 cm (3-inch) squares topped with brandy cream as a dessert.

*quantity of pâte brisée for
    25 cm (10-inch) container
    (page 65)
4–5 tablespoons mincemeat*

*50 g (2 oz) butter
50 g (2 oz) caster sugar
1 egg
75 g (3 oz) self-raising flour*

*grated zest and juice of 1
    orange
icing sugar for dusting*

MAKES 12–15 SQUARES   **OVEN TEMPERATURE 190°C**

METHOD Preheat the main oven to 190°C. Grease a swiss roll tin of approximately 18 × 25 cm (7 × 10 inches) and line with the pastry. Spread the mincemeat in a thin layer over the pastry base.

Cream the butter and caster sugar together until light and fluffy. Beat in the egg. Stir in the flour, orange zest and enough orange juice to make the sponge mixture a soft consistency.

Spread the sponge mixture very carefully over the mincemeat. Bake for 30–35 minutes. When cold dust with icing sugar.

NOTE This can be made in advance and frozen until Christmas.

Index to Recipes